Ordinary
and Sacred
As Blood:

Alabama women speak

Ordinary

and Sacred

As Blood:

Alabama women speak

Best wishes!
Van Potter

Mary Carol Moran

editor

With the hope
these pages bring
hours of pleasure
Enjoy!
Mary Carol Moran

Cover photos: front top, relative of J.J. Culver
                front bottom, family of Natasha Trethewey
                back, Helen Blackshear (age 4) and Mammy

Copyright 1999 by River's Edge Publishing Company, L.L.C.

Individual authors retain all rights to their material. Pages 241-2 give the publishing and award history of the poems and stories in this volume.

Publisher's Cataloging-in-Publication Data

Moran, Mary Carol
    Ordinary and sacred as blood: Alabama women speak / edited by Mary Carol Moran
    ISBN   0-9672676-0-9 (trade paper)
    1. Anecdotes.   2. Alabama Authors–Women.   3. Poetry.
    4. Interpersonal relations.   I. Moran, Mary Carol 1950-
    II. Title
158.2   99-63719

River's Edge Publishing Company, L.L.C.
907 4th Place SW
LaFayette, AL 36862

Text Design by Mary Carol Moran

Cover Design and Artwork by J.J. Culver
culvergraphics@mindspring.com

Preface

When my daughters were young, they loved to receive what they dubbed a "bag-o-wonders." The concept is similar to a Christmas stocking, a collection of small, useful, fun or interesting items, except that the bag-o-wonders can appear at any time. Even though they're in university now, I still surprise them with perhaps a box of granola bars, a sponge, some purple nail polish and a book of stamps. The fun for me is in the collecting, and in the pleasure the bag-o-wonders always elicits.

This book is my bag-o-wonders for you. Women from Gulf Shores to New Market, from high schoolers to great-grandmothers, from housewives and doctors to professors and retired accountants, have generously contributed their writing. Their words are funny, outrageous, poignant or pointed, and always genuine.

As with the bag-o-wonders for my children, I have enormously enjoyed collecting these poems and stories. I have had the opportunity to read over 1000 pieces of honest writing, of which my favorite 132 poems and stories are presented here. I hope they will give you much pleasure. Open the book, pull out a treasure, and enjoy!

Acknowledgments

Ordinary and Sacred As Blood: Alabama women speak, the premier (ad)venture of River's Edge, could not have come to be without the help of many, far too many to mention here. Throughout the process of developing, soliciting, collecting, choosing, and producing, I have met wonderful women from all over Alabama and made many new friends.

My first thanks go to the seventy-five gifted Alabama women writers who generously contributed their work to this book.

Several offered extraordinary help and inspiration. Susan Luther spread the word across northern Alabama and allowed me to use a portion of her poem "Red Clay" as the title. Susan Murphy helped make the initial decisions that gave shape to the chapters. Carolyn Buchanan scanned manuscripts into the computer and Margie Nanson—future publisher—typed, scanned, and helped proofread (any remaining errors are my oversight).

For practical advice I turned to Randall Williams, publisher of The Black Belt Press, who generously gave me time- and money-saving answers to every question, even the ones I didn't know enough to ask. J.J. Culver, a recent graduate in graphics design from Auburn University, smiled a lot and coped with my inexperience as he created the outstanding cover design and artwork. Ryan McMurtry at Vaughn Printing, Inc. received a vial of Alabama red clay in my efforts to get the cover color just right—he's a patient man.

Lastly, I'm blessed in my family. My daughters Lynde and Margie, the original 'bag-o-wonders' girls, have been my enthusiastic cheerleaders and honest critics for many years. My husband Larry, recently acquired and amazingly tolerant, supports my crazy schemes with critiques, proofreading, hugs, sympathy and meals out as needed.

Thank you all.

Contents

Living and Working

Raising Children

Kinfolk

Enjoying Nature

Maw-Maw and Paw-Paw

Saying Goodbye

Moving On

Remembering

Mammy Was a Slave

Helen Blackshear
Montgomery, Alabama

Mammy came to us in 1911 when I was about to be born. In those days babies in our town were delivered in their mother's bedrooms, and lucky was the young matron who secured Mammy as a midwife. Mother grew so attached to Mammy that she persuaded her to stay on to nurse me and later my small brother who was born the following year.

Mammy could not read or write and did not know her exact age or birthday, just that she was in her teens "when the Mancipation came." She had no last name in her childhood, just Caroline, and her mother had been sold down the river when she was a small child. Her one recollection was of her mother's telling her she must always remember the name of her white father, Green Watley, who was a young shoemaker on the plantation. Mammy occupied our best upstairs bedroom for twenty-five years and was like a second mother to my brother and me and the two sisters who came some years later.

My parents were not churchgoers, and Mammy was deeply disturbed over our being brought up "like little heathens". Sometimes she took us to her own church, where we sat in the front row among the friendly smiles of her black friends, listening with delight to the singing. More often, however, before her rheumatic knees began to fail her, Mammy sternly marched us across town to our own Baptist church.

Mammy's simple faith was deep-rooted. She talked to God all day, usually out loud, and we had no doubt that He answered her.

"Dear Lawd," Mammy would say, turning her eyes upward, "you see dis chile, how she actin'? Make her behave herself, Lawd!" To support the pleas to the ever-present Lord, she would sometimes remove her false teeth — which she often carried in her apron pocket anyway, as they did not fit well — and shake them at us. I am sorry to say that, as far as we children were concerned, these disembodied teeth were more effective than the appeals to the unseen Maker. When we became a little older, however, we would make a game of it and tease her.

Ordinary and Sacred As Blood

"Shake your teeth at us, Mammy," we would beg, "please, just once!" If she complied, we would run screaming from the room in pretended terror. Then we would laugh uproariously, Mammy loudest of all. Laughter was always close to the surface with Mammy, and though her aching knees induced long, pleading conversations with God or "blessed Jesus", she usually ended her complaints with a chuckle at herself.

"Blessed Jesus," Mammy would beg, "he'p me climb dese steps! Why you give me dese no 'count knees?" At the top of the offending stairs and seated finally in the armless rocking chair which in babyhood had comforted us all, Mammy would, as likely as not, burst into quavering but joyous song, in tune to the creaking of the rockers. "Will there be any stars, any stars in my crown... in that glo-o-rious home up above!" Mammy's heaven was a certain thing. It had crystal gates and golden streets, and the blessed cherubs were all the babies who had died.

In 1965, I self-published a book of reminiscences called *Mama Was a Rebel.* The popular chapter about Mammy led to an interesting series of events. When Mammy's granddaughter Stella died and her daughter Laura moved away, I never expected to hear from her family again. But word of my Mammy story spread among her numerous black friends, and they in turn wrote Mammy's knifolk in Indiana, Kansas, and Oklahoma.

First I received a letter from Marguerite Tomkins of Washington, D.C. She told me she was the granddaughter of Bama, one of Mammy's closest friends. A few days later I had a phone call from Tuscaloosa. A woman with a pleasant, well-modulated voice announced that she was Mrs. Ophelia Anderson, Mammy's granddaughter. This led to a wonderful visit from not only Ophelia but from her sister Theola, and two of Theola's daughters, Sue and Laura. The next surprise was a long letter from Ophelia's son, Dr. Collins F. Anderson, Jr., a retired dentist of Kansas City, MO. The most heart-warming result of all, for me, was to make contact again with Laura, Stella's daughter, an intelligent and fine-looking girl who had been a devoted nurse to Mammy during her last illness.

When I wrote my recollections of Mammy, my only thought was to keep my memories of her alive because I loved her. I never dreamed my story would serve as a catalyst to bring Mammy's scattered descendents together and give them added pride in their heritage.

The Smell of Cotton

B. *Kim Meyer*
Athens, Alabama

In honor and memory of my grandfather, Joel Swanner.

I still dream the smell of cotton
fresh-picked, as sweet as bouquets of
starched white angels
long rows he planted ages gone
the hot sun baking the lot of us
the old board wagon,
once-red sides balding now as
the tall brown man who could
pick three hundred pounds a day
I loved the long cool sacks
polk-berried names across one end and
fingers still purple come quitting time
bellies beaded blue or green
crawling behind each picker like some
self-righteous hungry snake
engulfing all the cotton we could
fill his belly with

So long the hours, during the noon break
we'd sometimes drag a sack
beneath the low-tide wagon
sea foam cotton slowly filling it
a knotty, lumpy bed with seeds
tomorrow's promise
to rest upon in the dormant air
sweat moving past our ears like
thoughts, or the small songs others sang
gospel seeping from their veins like heat

Ordinary and Sacred As Blood

Evening was a welcome time of work complete
the snake-sacks purged of their white bounty
after being hung on the rusty scale
guilty conquered victims for us to applaud
and Granddad tallying figures
each picker's weight scratched onto
brown cardboard in his spidery scrawl
pay shelled out in precious coins
worn folded bills from a tin box
into brown calloused hands
We all wandered home; dusty, tired
with aching hands, backs bent
perhaps to dream the same cotton smell

Tanessee's Daughter

Rachel Smith Sykes
Huntsville, Alabama

December 21, 1839

Dear Charlotte,

I want to tell you about our way of life here at Willstown in Alabama and tell you about the changes that have come to our people. For days after my father's good friend, James, brought me here from the overhills of Tennessee, I was distressed. I had grieved so much for my father and for the people of Tanessee that I found myself not caring whether I would be caught by the soldiers or not. My father felt that the Adairs would be kind to me and supportive of my culture. He wanted me to be brought up as a Cherokee.

Though I was not on "the Trail of Tears", I grieved for my friends, my family, and for my homeland. Perhaps it would have been best if I had gone to Oklahoma and if I were with Cherokee families. At first there were the urgent meetings and discussions about my being placed with the Adair family at Willstown. My father, who is a Cherokee warrior, had understood that I would stand a better chance with the family who had five strong sons than being on a forced march to Oklahoma.

Here at Willstown the men work the fields and hunt and fish if they have any time left after their chores. The women are Mrs. Adair, Susan, and myself. Susan is a neighbor who works part-time as a cook for us. The women are responsible for keeping the house, cooking, making clothes, and cleaning. There is no time to pity myself because we work six days a week and on Sunday we attend church. Often on Sunday afternoons we stay at church and attend singing sessions.

The Adair men are all friendly towards me. They are kind and respectful to me. I gather that they do not know what to make of my presence in their home. I would like to be a well-respected Cherokee woman who is a good neighbor and who can make a living by spinning,

Ordinary and Sacred As Blood

weaving, and doing crafts. Here I know of no one who is interested in keeping the Cherokee traditions alive. A Cherokee woman will not be heard in this culture.

Charlotte, my family tried to help the settlers adjust to the wilderness. My Grandmother was the Beloved War Woman who had assisted the Patriots during the Revolutionary War in North Georgia. Then gold was found in North Georgia and some of the people we had helped wanted our homeland.

I tried to talk to my father about who my birth mother was. I asked, "Could I go to my birth mother's family?" I remember that he told me, "Your Mother's family was ashamed of my love for your Mother. I found your Mother shivering from the cold weather and hungry on the night that we raided the South Carolina settlements." Her home had been burned but when he saw her red hair and pretty blue eyes, he understood why my Grandmother had befriended the Patriots when the British soldiers came. After I was born, my father took my Mother back to a white family in South Carolina. I do not even know my Mother's name.

The night that I last saw my father we had crossed the Cherokee River and had found a cave where we could camp. The next morning my father was gone and I had been left with James, a young warrior from the Wolf Clan. He told me that my father had returned to see if he could help other Cherokee families to hide from the soldiers. If only I could have met the Chickamauga people who tried to stay in Alabama.

My only solution as I see it is to be needed wherever I am. I would like to help my people so I am asking the Adairs to send me to a school where I can learn to help my people. Will I be accepted if I stay here in Alabama? As I finish my letter to you, I bow my head and ask God to direct my path.

Your friend,

Belithia Kimbrell

Rachel Smith Sykes is a member of the Echota Cherokee Tribe of Alabama.

I Remember Trains

Helen Norris
Montgomery, Alabama

I remember trains
The way they screamed like women
In the night
And mourned away into the dark
But left a sorrow in our sleep
To haunt a dream.

I remember trains
The way they screamed like peacocks
In the night
And died away with distance
But left a shudder in the air
To haunt us with a memory
Of iridescent wings with golden
Eyes now blind and folded
Like the day.

But more they screamed like women
In the night.
I remember how they cried they were
Forsaken though it was they who left us
To the dark.

An Alabama Christmas

Charlotte Miller
Opelika, Alabama

It was a year that stayed in the minds of Americans for generations, for it was a year of bank runs and failures, of FDR in the White House, and a New Deal for the 'Forgotten Man'. On the little farm my parents sharecropped in Alabama, we knew little of the Depression, for things were much as they had always been—only worse, of course, for my Pa was one of those 'forgotten' men Mr. Roosevelt spoke of so often. We did not have much, and what we did have was worn and ragged and often patched, but it was clean and as well mended as any sharecropper's wife could keep it. I was seven years old that year, all arms and knees and spindly legs, not far different from the four other girls in our family, just the youngest of the stairsteps of hand-me-downs and fistfights. There was also Benny, of course, but he was a boy, and as such did not get hand-me-downs, for there was no one to hand-down to him.

My pa was a little man, thin and short, and bent even more by hard years of work and worry. He farmed and he bottomed chairs and he sold baskets, and worked harder than any human being I'd ever seen before or since, but, then again, I guess he had to, to put food in the mouths of a family of eight in those years.

They were hard times, but they were also good times, at least in memory. We were all together, fed and warm in that drafty old shack. We might not have had all we wanted, but my pa tried — oh, how he tried, and especially at Christmas.

Christmas then was not as it is now. There was no television, and the only radio we ever heard was in the small country store where we ran a yearly charge against our share of the cotton crop. We children knew little of toys and presents; Santa Claus was in the Depression, too, and his funds were as short as anyone else's in the country. Pa had had to plow under a part of the cotton that year, and the government check in payment of that plowing under had gone to the man we sharecropped for, as everything seemed to go to him. It would be a sparse Christmas — but try to tell that to a seven-year-old.

That year I wanted a doll, not a hand-made doll put together from quilt scraps like I already had, the one my mama had made for me years before, but a store-boughten doll, like the ones I'd seen in the Sears and Roebuck catalog, or at the store, or on the rolling-store of a peddler's wagon that came by the house every so often. I had all the faith in the world that doll would be mine as I wrote my letter to Santa Claus the week before Christmas, for I knew he would not fail me. My list was long: stick candy and apples; and oranges, for I loved oranges; some mittens I'd seen at the store; and my doll of course. I showed what I had written to no one. It would be a secret until Christmas morning, shared with no one but Santa Claus. I gave my list to Pa to mail, and knew that my secret was safe.

The day before Christmas, Pa started for the store near where we lived, his arms laden down with eggs, baskets he'd woven from white oak splits, peach preserves, and even a hand-pieced quilt my mama had made for sale. I trailed along a few steps behind, but that morning Pa would not let me idle my time looking at all the wondrous things the storekeeper owned for sale; he sent me back out into the chill air to play, watching me until he knew the door had closed securely between me and the interior of the store. It seemed a long time before he came out, a long time as I wandered about the store yard, watching the few automobiles that trailed down the hard-packed clay road, my mind busily at work on dreams of the wondrous day to come.

When the door opened and Pa finally started out, Mr. Hardnett, the storekeeper, was just behind him. There was a peculiar expression on Pa's face, and both his voice and the voice of the storekeeper were raised as if they were arguing—I kept my distance and watched, seating myself on the running board of a conveniently-situated Model T, unable to make out what they were saying, and knowing better than to butt into the affairs of the grownups.

Pa had a small bundle in his hands, a small bundle wrapped in brown paper and tied with a string, the contents of which I knew he would have traded for in exchange for the eggs, preserves, baskets, and quilt we had brought to the store. Pa's mind seemed little concerned with the contents of the bundle at the moment, however, though my seven-year-old curiosity was almost overwhelmed at the sight. His eyes were instead on the thing the storekeeper held in his hand, a round, perfect orange, which Mr. Hardnett proceeded to slowly, and it seemed almost deliberately, peel and eat as they argued, letting the peelings fall to his feet there on the wooden flooring of the porch. I watched, my mouth watering, my eyes filled with the sight—oh, how I could hardly wait until tomorrow, when I could have my Christmas oranges, as well as the other presents Santa Claus would bring.

Pa stood on the store porch for a long time after the storekeeper had gone back inside, his face angry, his eyes set on something a far distance down the road, something I could not see even when I turned to look. After a time his gaze dropped toward his feet, and then he knelt, and it seemed for a time that he was praying. When he straightened, I thought I saw something in his hand, but it was quickly gone. He turned, his eyes finally settling on me where I sat at a distance across the yard on the running board of the Model T.

"Com' on, Vernie. It's time t' go home," he called, coming down the steps before the store.

That night I hardly slept at all, for visions of Santa Claus and presents and Christmas. It seemed I had only closed my eyes when suddenly it was daylight and my sisters were bounding over me on the bed we shared, trying to get to the other of the two rooms of our house, to the Christmas tree there, and the presents waiting for the family. I could hardly get to the tree for the sisters and the brother beneath it, all tearing eagerly into stockings, grabbing up this prize and that. When I finally reached my stocking where it hung from the mantlepiece, I found it filled with nuts and apples, and a stick of candy visible at the top. Beneath the tree were my mittens, and a new doll quilt and remade dress, but there was no store-boughten doll, and my oranges were nowhere to be found. I looked and looked, my heart sinking because I knew that Santa Claus had failed me—and then I saw a folded scrap of brown paper tied with a string to a lower limb of the Christmas tree. As I took it I saw my name printed on it, and the slowly made out words: "Times is hard, little one. Santa Claus does the best he can. Love to you on Christmas. S. Claus."

For a moment I stared at the paper. Then my eyes settled on the small pile of orange peels beneath the Christmas tree, and I began to smile. I might not have gotten my doll, but I had gotten a personal letter from Santa Claus, and I'd also given him something in return. I reached down to pick up one of the orange peels, smiling to myself. Next year I would leave a couple of Mama's teacakes on a plate beneath the tree. Maybe then Santa would eat the teacakes, and leave the oranges to me.

Shacks on Highway 231,
Along the High Red Clay Embankments

Bonnie Roberts
Huntsville, Alabama

These words are for those who never wrote a word,
or sang a song,
or thought a great thought,
or invented something,
or made something lasting.
These words are for those who lived
extraordinary non-extraordinary lives,
of getting up each day,
and walking through the day,
kicking at dirt clods, or
staring at trees,
or whittling a branch they finally
threw away
and of going to bed every night
with the hope of something better
or maybe without any hope at all.
These words are for those who simply lived,
whose lives are the poetry of existence
better than I can ever write
in my desire to leave something lasting,
in my desire to be remembered.
The old black men in felt hats
who played plastic checkers and waited in line
for the rubbery welfare cheese that was really
quite good, yellow and salty,
and the oily peanut butter stuck in their
kinky-pure cotton stalk beards.
Or the hook-nosed old maid waitress
who worked at the same burger grill

for thirty-five years.
Her black hair greasy and flattened beneath her cap,
she felt safe in sameness and
air-conditioned coolness,
her snowflake fingerprints melting away on the stainless counter.
Or the woman who tried to show her breasts to girls in the concrete
    bathroom at the Lauderdale County fair.
Or the fat man who collected coke bottles and was run down by a train.
Or the dirty girl in orange polyester shorts who disappeared from her
    yard two hours after she painted her toenails pink.
Or the husband and wife who never spoke of love but made love in the
    dark.
Or the failed auto-mechanic who spit tobacco juice in his dead grand-
    ma's withered face.
Or the young man with the cleft palate who longed to be a preacher.
Or the boy who washed his face with plain soap and water every
    morning at exactly the same time, and went to bed by the sun, every
    day.

They have all been forgotten.
They are more dead than dead.
But, here, their houses remain,
shadowing, overpowering any words,
these unwritten poems falling down
into artistic ruins
that belong in history books,
and in song books
because there are trees growing around the houses,
encircling the meaning of their inhabitants' lives,
singing in leaves, little twigs, and crooked stems
the green whistlings of unnoticed people, birds, and red summer dust,
and there are rivers full of paint rock running past the houses,
washing and coloring their lives clean of emptiness or pain or sin or
    want,
and the sky covers their remains with the deep blue breath
of the universe
and marks, inhales into its eternal mouth,
these perfect
perfect lives.

A Visit From Dr. Perkins

Frances Cleary Wittmeier
Orange Beach, Alabama

A pallid wisp of man
aged, delicate
leaving the world
in a slow shedding of dust.
An apparition, clad in black.
A serge suit worn to grayness.
His cracked satchel,
like an elephant's hide
embedded with dust
camouflaging what once
was black.
From within it's cavity
he extracts a set
of ludicrous teeth.
His admonishment's
more about digestion,
it seems. "Chew your food
until it is like warm sweet
milk." Southerners all,
we understand the term.
Our too broad smiles are
hidden behind hands.
He comes to "Talk to the children."
Strapping teens, past the wonder
we once had, for the gigantic teeth
and the shrinking man.
Too self-centered to understand
the need to be of service, by the
kind and gentle wisp of man.

High Adventure in "The Free State of Winston County"

Jessie Sherer Abbott
Jasper, Alabama

Nope, we are not a band of gypsies, but I *was* born in a tent located at a road construction campsite in Winston County, Alabama, locally called "The Free State of Winston."

My mother, Jessie Sherer, was a small woman, five feet three inches tall, with heavy black hair that reached half way to her waist, but she always wore it in a bun at the nape of her neck. She had snapping brown eyes that at times appeared to be black. My Dad, Clint Sherer, Sr., was a big six-footer with black hair and a pair of eyes that looked as if a piece of the bluest of skies had dropped into his face.

When Mother and Dad were first married, Dad was working for the Southern Railway. In 1916 the railroad was always having layoffs, and when this happened to Dad, he was fortunate to find a road construction job in Winston County. This meant that Dad would get home only on some of the weekends.

Even though I was already on the way, Mother said, "I did not marry your Dad to have him live one place and me another. If he goes, then I go." So, Mother moved to the campsite. Before I was due, Mother was to come back to Jasper and stay with her sister until after the big event. But I decided to make my appearance early, in a tent!

During those years Dad would be called back to the railroad, where he worked for a few months until there was another layoff. Each time he was laid off, he was always fortunate to go back to a road construction job. During these back-and-forth years, one of my sisters and one of my brothers were born in tents at road construction camps.

About ten miles of road at a time would be surveyed and the campsite would be set up at or near the five-mile marker. At the center of the construction campsite was a self-sufficient unit of a commissary, a dining hall, a cook shack, living quarters (tents) for all the men and their families, a blacksmith shop, a tool shed, a corral for the horses and mules, and sheds for feed, large equipment, and buggies and wagons and such. When the ten miles of road were completed, the campsite would be moved another ten miles along the route, and work would continue.

Our living quarters were two tents, sixteen feet by sixteen feet, put together back-to-back so that the end flaps could be raised or dropped for privacy. The flooring was made of rough, wide, splintery planks and the walls were built of the same type of planks, about three feet high. After this the top frame was built to the regular height of a cabin and attached where the walls left off. Then the tents were draped over the framework and fastened to the top of the planked-up walls assuring us a cozy home. We had a wood-burning heater, and firewood was never a problem, because there was a whole forest just for the taking. I don't ever remember being cold in the winter once we were inside the tents and had a good fire going.

Clint Jr., my oldest brother, and I learned to use a big crosscut saw that was bigger than either one of us. I still have a scar on my right hand as a souvenir from my wood-cutting days. Howard and Elsie (brother and sister), had the job of stacking the wood with the help of toddler, Cowboy, pitching in to do his share by bringing up a stick of wood to be stacked along with theirs.

We lived so far out in the forest that there was absolutely no outside entertainment. Television had not been invented and the radio was almost unknown. With so many in our family, we never lacked for someone to play games with. Elsie and I were just as much boys as our brothers were. They wouldn't play our sissy games so we usually had to play theirs.

But on Saturday nights we did have entertainment. One large tent in the center of the camps was set aside as a central gathering place. The men had built benches out of rough lumber all around the sides of the tent, and small tables that were placed around in front of the benches. At the time, there were games of checkers, dominoes or set-back being played. One of the men had built a battery-powered radio to be used on Saturday nights only, when we listened to the first year of the "Grand Ol' Opry."

Other entertainments were the get-togethers at the different family tents. One event happened at our tent that I'll never forget. I saw it with my very own eyes, but even now, almost 70 years later, I'm not quite sure that I believe it. It's for sure that I cannot explain it, but it really happened.

Ordinary and Sacred As Blood

There was a lot of excitement at our tent that evening. Supper was finished in a hurry and all the chores were completed in no time flat. A group of neighbors came over, saying they could make a table walk and talk. A small table with chairs around it was set in the middle of the floor. Mother, Dad and their friends sat around it with their thumbs touching and their little fingers touching the person's little finger next to them.

One of the men did all the talking. He told everyone that regardless of what happened they were not to move their hands. They could stand up, but never break the connection of fingers touching. Once the fingers were moved, it was all over — the table would drop like a stone.

The man talked to the table as if it were a person. He gave it instructions: he said it would only be given questions that could be answered with a "yes" or "no" or numbers. If the answer was "yes," the table was to tap twice and if the answer was "no," then it was to tap once.

I'm sure it didn't, but to us kids, it seemed to take hours. Once in our lives we were speechless. Finally, the table started to tilt, raising one leg and tapping on the floor with it. The man started asking questions: like give the age of each person named. Other questions were asked that could be answered with a yes or no, and each time, the table tapped the right answers. We even asked how many mules were in the corral. Dad was the only one who knew the answer to that one, so after the table tapped out the number, the others asked Dad if that was right. He had to admit that the table had tapped out the right number.

Of course there were scoffers in the group. Men even crawled under the table trying to find strings or wires attached to the legs of the table. A couple of the men decided that they were going to hold the legs of the table to the floor when a question was asked. Regardless of how much strength they exerted they could not keep the table from tapping out the answers.

When the group made the table walk across the floor, all the chairs were moved back, and the ones with their hands on the table had to walk along with the table. Finally the connection of hands was broken. As soon as the connection was broken, the table dropped, and that was the end of that little episode. Down through the years, I've seen people look askance at us and almost (notice I said almost) call us out-and-out liars. But I still say I saw it happen.

Recall — The Inexpensive Sport

Madge Pfleger
Mobile, Alabama

To bestir the memory is like trying to put a butterfly into a jar using one finger — very delicate labor. When its return is triggered by some current event, it can quickly spread backward in directions not necessarily to our bidding.

The mood of the early thirties was uncertain, sad, and often angry. The frustration of the men, unable to find work, drove many to alcoholism, some to suicide, and many more to abandonment of their families. For these men, riding the rails could literally be a deadly experience; overly tired hobos would often fall asleep, lose their grip, and fall beneath the wheels of the train. I vividly recall such a happening.

My father was then an agent for the L & N Railroad. Late one afternoon while I was at the depot waiting to walk home with him, such an incident occurred on the rails immediately outside the station. Overwhelming noise from the passage of the freight train covered any outcry there might have been as well as the initial commotion of the rail crew's discovery of the man thrown alongside the tracks. As the freight cleared the area, sounds of excited activity drew me to the depot waiting room where, working together, the crew had carried the legless body of a mutilated hobo.

I remember the weather was bitingly cold and the pot-bellied stove was glowing red with its fire. As dusk came early at that time of year, two hanging kerosene lanterns were already lit. Not knowing what else to do, the men had propped the injured man up, his back against the wall, with what remained of his legs stretched before him. Several members of the crew had returned outside to retrieve the missing legs before dark.

As an eight-year-old, I had no understanding of shock, so was dumbfounded that, while his life blood was pulsing away, he only asked for a cigarette. He seemed unconscious of any pain. Oddly enough, even now, tangled with the details of the horror there remain the unrelated facts that his eyes were brown and we never knew his name.

20   *Ordinary and Sacred As Blood*

Using the telegraph, my father notified the authorities in Mobile of the accident. As the fastest of ambulances could travel no more than thirty miles an hour, well over an hour passed before help finally arrived. In 1930, ambulance personnel were not so fortunate to have the sophisticated life-support systems now common to most emergency units. We were notified later — again by telegraph — that the accident victim had not survived the trip to the hospital.

It was not all negative in the thirties. The air was clean and the loudest noises were from neighborhood dogs barking at the rare passing of an automobile or the newest baby crying in the next room. Couples held on for dear life dancing to music from heavy wax records turning on hand-cranked Victrolas and the radio was a living room fixture uncoupled with a video screen.

Instant foods were the ones gathered ripe from the garden with the warm sun smell and taste about them. Usually there were just three cereal choices on the grocery shelf — oatmeal (only one natural flavor), Cream of Wheat, and a wheat bran. Hershey kisses were ten for a penny, soda pop was a nickel, and fast food was a quick peanut butter and jelly sandwich eaten at the kitchen table.

The process of looking backward in memory is unique; in so doing you are both bystander and participant. Some memories become blurred and resist recall, while others, like mine of the mutilated hobo, remain in focus, totally unwelcome, but there in permanent ink. You may be on center stage or on the other side of the footlights giving applause, but the past is always there and it belongs to you.

Wounded Visitor : World War II

Estel M. Dodd
Arab, Alabama

We huddled near the small
coal-burning fireplace,
backs turned to the wind which
seeped through loose windowsills
while outside, snow glistened
with moonglow
and trees stood tall and black,
sentries in leadened Alabama sky.

Mama worked quietly
in the nearby kitchen, glancing
at the door, the undraped windows,
as if she saw or heard beyond
our lamp-lit boundaries.

When the knock came, she hesitated
only slightly, glanced at us children,
then turned the knob to a rush
of icy wind.

Silhouetted in the doorway's glow,
he stood trembling
coatless, hatless, wounded
and though Mama didn't know
if he meant to do us harm
she asked him in —
for she had seen his torn
and grimy pants leg,
caked dark blood on his cold-blue knee...

His wool uniform steamed
as it dried before the fire,
his hair dripped rivulets
of snow-melt down stubbly cheeks,
his chapped hands shook
as he stretched them to the warmth.

While Mama gave him coffee
and a plate of buttered bread
my brother inched his way close
to the fire-tongs, just in case
he needed to protect us from this
stricken, shivering soldier.

He seemed as nervous as we were,
as though he could not spot his enemies —
and soon, mumbling thanks to Mama,
asked directions to the highway
and stumbled out into the snowy haze.

He did not see the clothesline
in the orchard, stretched
between the front porch and the road,
and when it caught him in the throat
flipping him backward in the snow,
he lay there whimpering
for but a moment —
then slowly stood, staggered
through the orchard to the road
and disappeared.

We heard nothing more of this man
who lost his way that cold,
cold night —
whether he lost his war,
or the war lost him.

The Medicine Show

Jane Allen
Wetumpka, Alabama

When I first met Maggie Allen, my mother-in-law, I soon discovered she was a born storyteller and, through the years, I became an avid listener. She especially enjoyed telling about the personal experience she and her husband, Milton, or "Red" for short, had shared with Hank Williams before he became famous.

Maggie and Red had always loved to listen to the heart-wrenching music of Hank and his band, the Drifting Cowboys, and now they were coming to Goshen, a little town south of Montgomery, Alabama. It was 1945, and Hank was traveling with a medicine show that would be in the community for a whole week. Hank would sing many of his own songs, and then the show would offer extra-added attractions which appealed to these down-home folks.

Maggie could hardly wait — she didn't get out much, what with raising six kids, working at the sewing factory in nearby Troy, and helping Red in the fields. She would wear her brand-new frock that she had made from a beautiful flowered feed sack, and Red would wear his khaki shirt and pants and brown felt hat with the wide band. Maggie decided they would take the children with them as a special treat.

Finally, Saturday night arrived and Hank fulfilled all their expectations. They were thrilled to the bones to see and hear Alabama's 'own' in person. Maggie and Red had always thought Hank was the best country and western singer on the radio, and now he proved to be even a greater talent in the flesh because of his gentle, soulful eyes and expressive singing style. The words he wrote came from deep within his heart, as he turned his tangled emotions inside out, exposing his inner feelings to the receptive crowd.

The show's special feature this particular night was a nail driving contest open to anyone in the audience. The man or woman who could drive six nails into a 2 by 4 in the shortest time would win a whole dollar bill -- a lot of money in those days.

Ordinary and Sacred As Blood

Maggie shouted bravely from the crowd, "I'll try."

Her friends and neighbors didn't laugh because they knew she had always worked just as hard as any man in the whole countryside and was strong as an ox. She had plowed their mule "Pet" for years, dug deep holes for fence posts, and nailed fencing wire to the posts. Why, she could drive nails along with the best of them!

She looked at her sun-baked hands and approached the flatbed of the Model-T Ford with an air of confidence.

"Ready, set, go," hollered Hank excitedly.

Maggie hammered and hammered with great strength and, in a few minutes, won the contest hands-down. Hank gleefully proclaimed her the winner, gave her the crisp bill, and tenderly kissed her on the cheek. Maggie's face turned bright red, almost the color of her hair. She knew this would always be a night to cherish.

It was during this particular visit that Hank was locked up in the local jail for drinking in public, which inspired him to write the song, "One-Eyed Sheriff." Ironically, rumors later circulated around Goshen that the sheriff sold him the whiskey in the first place!

As Hank gained fame at the Grand Ole Opry and nationally, Maggie and Red heard that he continued to drink heavily. Perhaps the pressure of being a big star was just too much for this deeply rooted Southern boy. Maggie and Red just chose to recall that Hank once came to Goshen with a lively medicine show, sang some moving songs about life's joys and sorrows, and gave a country woman a delightful memory that lasted a lifetime.

Pairing Off

blind date

lauren kenney
Auburn, Alabama

it was all-you-can-eat ribs night.
words flapped from my mouth
like disoriented pigeons on a pilgrimage
and smashed into the plastic bib
he had tucked into his collar.
i looked away politely
while my awkward attempt at conversation
drowned in Porky's secret sauce.

he didn't seem to mind.
he asked if i was finished
and reached across the table
to take the food from my plate,
to consume all-i-could-not-eat.
later, when he vultured toward my head
to collect a goodnight kiss,
my lips and eyes slammed shut.

The Highwayman

Frances Cooper Smith
Montgomery, Alabama

My heart's an inn beside the way,
And love is tenant for the night,
And nothing I can do or say
Can haste or stay him in his flight.

When morning comes he will be gone,
And none may call him back — so we
Can only wait and ponder on
How long a night this night may be.

I tell you this that you may know,
And knowing may come back no more...
My heart's an inn beside the way,
And love has come and gone before.

Kudzu Grows Twelve Inches A Day

Evelyn Ryan
Harvest, Alabama

I guess I shoulda known it would mean trouble when I bought that red dress for Faye Nell. The thing is, though, she's so beautiful — really beautiful — that I can't stand it when her blue eyes get all big and soft and her mouth is open just a little like she's tasting heaven. She was just standing in front of the big window, looking, when I walked by. Like always, I slowed to look at the sweetest shape in Anderson county, the soft curls the color of crusty biscuits, the perfectness of Faye Nell. 'Course, I knew she wasn't smart, or what most people called good, but she was like the first day of the best summer you ever had.

So, I took her inside the store, and enjoyed the pop-eyed face of the uppity clerk when I told her "We want that dress in the window," and pulled out a big roll of bills, all fifties.

The dress was three hundred, a high price for feeling so good for a little while, but worth every penny. That roll went back five years, long years of growing Willie Ben Husted's pot, in places where nobody knew to look, hiding the gathered crop where nobody knew to find it.

Just like I was sure she would, Faye wore her new dress that Saturday night to the Dew Drop Inn. Too bad she didn't have anybody much to see the show, just the usual beer-swilling crowd of rednecks, but there was one who hadn't missed a lick, somebody who'd sell his grandma if he had a buyer. Instead of cutting up on the dance floor, Faye Nell in her red dress was at a table by the corner window, talking low and serious with Willie Ben. Standing outside in the shadows by the window, I could hear him say "So, in the morning, me and you will take the bus to Mobile, and will meet the man from the movie producer. In a little while, you'll be on your way to Hollywood. How's that?"

I knew about the man "from Hollywood". Two other girls from our little town, girls dumb, country and pretty like Faye Nell, had gone to Mobile to meet him, and had never been seen or heard from again. A real beauty would be a hot property for him.

I waited outside till nearly midnight, when Willie Ben started home, weaving and very unsteady on his feet from the bunch of double whiskeys he'd had. I followed till he got to the darkest part of the path along the cypress slough. There was a half moon, enough light for what I was to do. Years of knowing that if I missed my shot at a rabbit or squirrel I missed supper, paid off. The little .22 in my pocket was easy to hide— nobody knew I carried it, and a shot in Willie Ben's left eye caused little noise or blood. The dark water covered him quickly, and the hanging screen of vines would hide it all in a short time. Everybody knew Willie Ben had started home drunk, and in a few days or weeks they'd identify him by his front gold tooth and that would be the end of it.

The next morning my friend John C. came by my house and sat down by me on the front steps. "Billy," he says, "do you know old man Stacy's done sold that land where the slough is to some folks that's gonna drain it and build a store?"

Now I'm counting my roll to see if it's enough to get to Mexico. Kudzu grows twelve inches a day, but that ain't enough to help me now.

Pyramids

lauren kenney
Auburn, Alabama

Mathematicians in ancient Egypt knew
that humans could build mountains.
They experimented as they built
and on their first attempt at Meidum
they started up at too steep an angle
from too narrow a base
so that when they got right past the middle
it crumbled under the pressure
of its own weight.
Maybe they should have stopped then.
Instead they married their flawless architecture
to the principles of physics.
By the birth of Cheops they knew
how humans could build mountains.
2.3 million blocks of granite
were cut from the escarpment
that overlooks Gizeh
and dragged across miles of desert
to the edge of the plateau.
Each was chiseled down so that
when placed side by side,
a breath
could not squeeze through
the spaces between them.
Stone by stone,

the layers piled up
until it was complete.
Satisfied with the masterpiece,
Cheops watched his tomb
until he died.
He was mummified then interred
beneath five million tons
of exact stone.
I think of the way you love me
with such monumental precision
and I know how dead kings feel.

The Black Widow

Angelynne Amick McMullan
Birmingham, Alabama

She kills
in life
giving

resplendent
in her
blackness

alluring
in her
timeless red.

His flesh will
nourish her eggs
the bearers of his code.

They couple
death
with
life

free to be
not soulmates

no contemplating
battle lines
or searching
for love connection.

She weaves
her perfect tapestry.

He teeters
on
her web.

Ordinary and Sacred As Blood

Rage

Marilyn Hunt-Lewis
Huntsville, Alabama

I pray
never to see yr face again
awake or asleep.

I fear
filling the hole in my life
with yr blood.

stuffing yr words
back in yr mouth
and lighting a blow torch
to yr tongue.

breaking yr arms
with my fingernails
and stripping skin
the way men
strip clothes.

from yr waist down
I'll leave you intact
in a glass curio
so I won't forget
to hate what you've done
to send me through middle passages
utterly unable
to give my love.

Juice

Pippa Coulter Abston
Decatur, Alabama

Just to demonstrate
the transforming nature of love,
take peaches. She once
loathed them - the deep red
marrow too raw, too likely
to trickle down her chin -
a mockery of blood,
the province
of grinning teenage boys.
Even the peel was skin
breaking like the nappy cheek of a girl
beneath her teeth.

The day he left
she brought home ten -
one for every summer. When she bit,
at first gingerly
and then with the lawlessness
of hunger
if there were small screams, she didn't stop
until her throat filled
with the juice of absolution,
until it gushed
onto her chin. In the same
way one waits
to wash away ashes
or chrism oil or a first
kiss, she let it
dry.

The pits she laid as evidence
along the window, one clean row.

Ordinary and Sacred As Blood

In a Land That Is Fairer Than Day

Ramey Channell
Leeds, Alabama

> There's a land that is fairer than day
> And by faith we can see it afar,
> For the Savior waits over the way
> To prepare us a dwelling place there.
>> "In the Sweet By and By," S.F. Bennett, 1867

The two old people lay side by side on the sagging bed, a rumpled sheet kicked down to the foot of the iron bedstead. The old man was wearing a white sleeveless undershirt and boxer shorts given to him by a daughter or son many years ago. He lay flat on his back with one hand on his bony chest.

The old woman lay on her side with her back to him. She was even smaller and thinner than her husband, and she made a dry, raspy sound when she breathed. She had been sick for about two years and wasn't expected to last much longer, but her husband took care of her and waited on her patiently.

He knew his children didn't like her. They were all grown now, and had families of their own; didn't come around too often. At Christmas and on his birthday his oldest son would bring the babies to see him. And usually they'd sit out in the swing on the front porch because their mother had told them not to go inside the house anymore; they might catch what the old woman had.

But the two little girls would sing a song for Papa, and dance a tap-dance on the rough wooden porch, and shyly hand him some little present they had brought him. Sometimes they'd step inside the dark little house, into the front room where the old couple slept. The smell was sweet and holy to them: old apples, tobacco, hair tonic, pine wood and leather. It smelled like Papa.

And he tried to give them what he could. He gave them honey from the two dilapidated bee hives behind the house, and radishes that tasted like the earth from the little garden. He took them for a ride in the old wagon;

Alabama women speak

37

that was before he'd sold the mule. He taught them to hang a tea strainer or fly swatter outside the back door because all the little holes would puzzle the "Booger-man" and keep him out. And he showed them his treasured nail keg full of marbles, letting them dig in with their little soft brown hands.

"Get you a handful," he told them, laughing at their excitement. "Pick you out some purty ones."

That was just a short while after Nettie died.

That's why they resented Eller, his pore little woman who lay beside him now. He'd married her too soon after Antoinette died. He knew.

But it was done now. Maybe they would have all learned to accept her over time, if she hadn't took sick this way. Now that made them resent her even more, and he knew they shook their heads and repeated the story of how he'd brought her home with him, sitting up on the wagon seat beside him.

Well, she was a pretty little thing then, like a little bird perched up beside him. Her skin was pale and thin looking, and her wispy twist of hair as white as cotton. And she smiled, right proud to be courted by that tough, dark skinned old man, not much taller than she was.

He remembered the pain of losing Nettie, and the grieving kids on the day she was buried. But, he didn't want to live alone, so he took peaceful, nervous little Eller to be his wife too soon.

She lay sleeping beside him now, in the dark, humid July night. What dreams she had, he didn't know. She was so close to crossing over, she must have dreamed of Heaven — "in a land that is fairer than day." The doctors said there wasn't a thing could be done.

He slept with his mouth open, lost in dreams of the old times, the old place, up on the mountain. The summers and the winters. The younguns being born and growing up.

He'd been mean and ornery in his younger days. And he'd get drunk and get into fights, and scare the kids. Well, they didn't know what to think of him then, just like they didn't know what to think of him now. But they were his folks, and they could forgive him, couldn't they?

They'd said he was too old to get married again. How could he stand to live with her, they asked, after being married to somebody as fine as Nettie? Well, Nettie was fine. And they had been together a long time...

married when they were just kids... the scrappy mean-as-a-snake half breed and the tall, beautiful blue-eyed Antoinette.

The old man dreamed of Nettie and Eller together. They were laughing, walking in a field of tall grass with the sun shining all around them like noon time. In a land that is fairer than day. Both of the women were holding wild flowers in their hands as they walked together, laughing, looking straight at him. Well, he thought he'd never seen the like; the two of them walking and laughing together, and looking so fine and strong. A sudden breeze blew across the tall grass, tugging at their soft cotton dresses and the flowers in their hands.

The fire began in the kitchen of the tiny wooden house, and the flames swept through the hot Alabama night. Arthur woke up next door and ran towards the horror of it — the dark and the monstrous fire devouring Uncle Reed's little house. His voice sounded all wrong to him, like somebody else's voice when he screamed.

"Uncle Reed! Uncle Reed! The house is on fire! Uncle Reed, get up! Oh, God. Oh, God."

And the brown skinned old man ran out the back door, in his old wrinkled underclothes, right into Arthur's arms. Smoke was everywhere and the heat was terrible, and the old man wasn't really awake. He looked up at Arthur's terrified face. Then, instantly, he was awake. He saw his house in flames and smelled the smoke and cinders, and began pulling away from Arthur.

"I'll have to get Eller!" the old man hollered. The terror was more than Arthur could stand, worse than the heat. He tried to hold onto the old man, and tried to tell him not to go. But he fought like a young man, and got away from him.

"I've got to get Eller," he hollered. And he went back in.

Tour of the Library, His and Hers

Pippa Coulter Abston
Decatur, Alabama

Here's Hemingway - Men
without Women, planning expeditions
in the rough
beyond, leaving hills

with curves like sprawling beasts
to come here, spine
to spine with Jane and all the Sense

she can call up. Next to him
she's tepid, a constricted
heart - all her brightest wit
gone brittle

Next to her his wandering's
maudlin, spareness
just a terse conceit

    but here by weather's mercy, seasons
    upon seasons wet and dry

they're joined; at his completion
she begins. Look quickly and you'll catch him

muddy boots beside her door,
playing anagrams at tea - she's
slipping out at midnight,
hip-deep in the big river

casting with an easy breath;

Listen - what they're telling now
is true, what we've come to-
learning the only story left us

line by line.

Now We Lay Us Down to Sleep

Helen Norris
Montgomery, Alabama

Now we lay us down to sleep.
Two craft in mothering waters moored,
And fathoms deep our cradling shadows
Lie. The moon is salted down
In sea and smells of brine. The freight
Of waking hours spills and drifts
To lap the land... There comes a long
Intake of breath, a yielding sigh,
As if the giant bird of prey
That haunts the day has closed his eye
And we are safe to close our own...
I feel you slip your moorings. I am
Humbled in the lone dominion
Of my waking. Then you draw
Me into dark. You drug me with
Your sleep, so secret and so grave
A thing it bears the scent of sin.
Together we are tarred with night...

And soon we sleep as sentinels
Against we know not what, each
One for the other one against
The undertow of dreams, against
The dark's unhallowing, against
The bird that haunts the night, the owl
Of death that calls our names, against
We know not what... and fathoms deep
Our shadow anchors lie.

Ordinary and Sacred As Blood

Passing the Peace

Evelyn Hurley
Gaylesville, Alabama

A spray of rubbery fern
and white plastic carnations
blooms on the peeling post
of the farm house porch.

Neighbor women approach
bearing baked alms before them,
exhausted pity in their eyes,
rehearsed sympathy in their throats.

"You'll be so lonely, Mable."

Mable turns age old eyes
to the peace lily
blooming just beyond the window,
listens down the years
of bourbon flavored days,
breathes the sour smell
of angry nights.

"There are worse things,"
she whispers,
"than being lonely."

The Words Unsaid

Frances Cooper Smith
Montgomery, Alabama

Now that the time has come I cannot grieve,
My grief already spent through many years,
Precisely measured, thin, and without tears
From that far time we first came to perceive
There was between us an enduring veil,
And tried in quiet and polite despair
To reach each other, finally aware
Our helpless words would only thrash and fail.

If I should grieve it's not that I shall miss
Your presence; I shall not be more alone
Without you than beside you, this I own.
If I should grieve my grief shall be for this:
The words unspoken in the quiet throat,
The cry unanswered and the heart remote.

No Guts, No Glory

Ora Dark
Auburn, Alabama

"No Guts, No Glory", the message appears on the computer screen automatically. Another pearl of wisdom to make you a better employee, but at six o'clock in the morning only the brown stuff in the foam cup can bring me back to this place. My hands grip the hot cup so it won't spill. I'll print out the screen so I can mull it over after my heart starts.

Kathy takes her place at the row of word processors for service order typists, all hooked up to the giant mainframe of BellSouth. I nod to her and sit down to perform my morning rituals. Every morning since the beginning of January, I've logged onto the screen that displays work orders for phone service in the New Orleans area, scrolling past the residential service till I come to business orders. After five weeks of wasting my time, jackpot!

"Dial-a-Sailor" flashes across the black screen. With a few quick taps on the keyboard, the service order comes into view. A ship called the *U.S.S.Courageous* will be at Pier II on February 20, and needs several lines and numbers. Quickly printing the privileged information, I tuck it in my canvas bag, under my banana. Kathy seems oblivious to our good fortune.

Kathy stands out as the breathtaking Amazon of the 11th floor of Canal Place One. People pause their world when they see her; she's used to it. Add the heavy seductive voice of a temptress, the sweet understanding of someone ancient, and throw in the wildest, loudest Cajun accent you've ever heard — she's the heart breaker package. We make a strange pair. Short and curvy, dark hair and blue eyes, I'm usually referred to as "cute". As roommates we compliment each other, but as a pair of single females, we're deadly.

Kathy moved in after Christmas, both of us vowing to give up eating, drinking, the lazy life of T.V. and shopping, as good as that is. Instead we turn our energies to exercise, saving money, and capturing men. The decision to move into my apartment seemed wiser than moving in with her, since her single mother and two single sisters live in the same house. You can't deny the air of obvious anxiety in that household. Too much Yin and not enough Yang if you know what I mean.

With 89 women on our side of the office and only 11 of them married, we feel a duty to blaze new trails in the field of progressive dating. We eliminated the bar scene; Kathy is a recovering alcoholic and I'm a cheap date. Our plans consist of all the usual tactics plus something new, ordering men by phone. What is better than a dreamboatful of more than 275 men anchoring two blocks from where we are? Odds of finding an enviable date for Mardi Gras will leapfrog in our favor.

****

"U.S.S. Courageous, this is not a secure line, can I help you sir or ma'am?" the voice stops quickly, catching me off-guard.

Every ounce of courage in my body helps my voice simulate composure, and femininity oozes out without any prompting. Almost as if something takes over automatically.

"Yes, you sure can help me. Is this the Dial-A-Sailor line?"

"Dial-A-Sailor? I'm not sure, ma'am. Who did you want to speak to?" the sailor on the other end of the line stammers.

"Is there someone there who can give me some information on getting a date for Mardi Gras?"

"Just a moment, ma'am, let me connect you with the duty officer. Hold on one moment, okay?" There is a click and for a moment, silence.

My body shakes, my heart bangs against my breastbone, beads of perspiration sting my face and my scalp starts itching. The phone becomes heavy and hot. My chest strains as if all the air has been sucked out of the room. I may laugh, cry, or hide in the closet. Maybe all of these.

By God, I'm not going to feel afraid, or weak or silly. This can't be any worse than ordering pizza, can it? It can't be worse than trying to pick out the right toppings. Or ordering the right size. What if it's too big, or too little? I suppose if you're hungry enough, you'll eat anything.

"This is Lieutenant Commander Mason, can I help you, ma'am?" This was an older voice, steady and without any nervousness.

"Yes, I thought I was calling the Dial-A-Sailor number. I would like

Ordinary and Sacred As Blood

to arrange for two officers for dates for Mardi Gras. Is that possible?"

I can hear people laughing, and other voices, but I've come too far now.

"Let me get the information and I'll have to call you back. Will that be all right?"

In the background I can just make out the words, "Dial-A-Sailor," being whispered over and over by the guys near the phone.

"Yes, I would like two officers, please, over thirty, single and one should be tall. My name is Faron Tway and my friend is Kathy Summers, my phone number is 525-6680. Thank you very much for being so patient. Do you think you might call by tomorrow?"

"Yes, ma'am, all the officers but myself and most of the crew are off the ship right now but I have some candidates in mind. I'll check with them in the morning. Can I call you about 8 o'clock?"

"Great, have a nice evening. I'll talk to you tomorrow." This is much simpler than ordering pizza, and they call when my order is ready. This is too easy. Will he really call me back?

Just as I put the receiver on the hook, the phone rings. Can it be the ship trying to verify if this is a prank call? What if he is already calling me back? I put on my most polite voice.

"Hello?"

excerpt from Ora Dark's first novel, *No Guts, No Glory*

Living

and Working

The Magic Vanilla Bottle

Anne George
Birmingham, Alabama

I have had the same bottle of vanilla for thirty-five years. It's a ten ounce bottle of Ann Page Pure Vanilla bought at an A&P that has been out of business for thirty. The threads are wearing in the metal cap and probably the contents aren't as pure as they should be. But there is no way I can replace it. My children, fast approaching middle-age with children of their own, check the bottle and marvel at it. It's magic, Mama's vanilla. The amount never goes down. No matter how many milkshakes or cakes we make, there the level is — right at the same place.

Is it possible that at the wedding at Cana someone sneaked out the back flap of the tent, bought some cheap wine and filled the good casks? Anybody checked the difference in the price of imitation and pure vanilla lately? Or thirty-five years ago? Anybody with a mother-in-law who thought imitation vanilla was no better than water? Anybody with children so dense they think the vanilla bottle stays full?

Sometimes when I take the bottle down and pour out a teaspoonful, my conscience twinges slightly, On the other hand, how many people are blessed with a miracle? Go figure!

Between the Tampax and the Doritos

Tina Harris
Montevallo, Alabama

Hey you
It has been awhile
We decide as we stop to talk
Of them and that and the other
And I wish I could say more.
Say that I admire you
I like your toughness
Blackness, your momness
Your laugh that rumbles out of some deep cavern in your chest
That I like all the nessness of you.

But we are between the tampax and the doritos
And I'm chicken to say it here
So I ask about your child and job
I laugh
And smile
Hoping you know.

Collaboration

Linda Frank
Huntsville, Alabama

We knew each other well. After all, we had been coming together for some years to explore the feminine spirit in all kinds of ways. This Alabama summer evening we were sitting by the water with the fragrance of roses, gentle music and candlelight, making it easy for the poems to emerge.

Each of us wrote a line and passed it to another, on and on, until together we had created eight poems each singing our collective heartsong.

1

The dawn is breaking, it will be a new day
The pink rimmed rock luminescence, snake like.
And the dance continues, through the light.
Mysteries unfolding to the song
The sun casts shadows in the rock; indigo, black, rust, gold are all
     present.
The piper pipes, creation awakens, life begins anew
Freshness of a new yellowed sky invites us to rise and participate
All that is required of us is the dance.

2

The waves swept across the ocean
Mother moon fingering each ripple
The blue-green sea foam gurgles delight
The fish swim with delight, their rainbow colors filling the void
The dolphins dance in the moonlight
A solitary whale holds on his back, an iridescent laughing mermaid
And the sounds sing sweetly on the wings of the wind in the night
As the sea responds in unending rhythm to the sounds of life

3

The blessings of the flute fills the air
with the songs of nature and of harmony
Alone I catch the solitary note
Great glass globes of translucent color
Float on the stillness of translucent sound and purple fills the night
Fuschia, orchid, and mauve color the sky.
Darkness brings the stars, moon and stillness to my heart.

4

The silken notes tumble down the solitary plain
Melodies that beckon my soul
Across the eons of time no words need be spoken
The soul whispers with the harmony of the spheres
And dances in the presence of awe
The notes move across my skin like fresh cool waters
Sparkling green and blue and purple in the silver flickers of clarity
Red and amber, chartreuse and orange tones that cloak the coyotes
    howl.

5

The pure clean arrow of flute song strips away the husks of my outside
    world
Mind loosens its hold that other worlds may enter
The yellow maize greets the golden goddess of light
And we all bow in delight to behold the fullness of the moon
Sounds of the night bring joy to my heart
There is harmony and balance and my soul feels at peace
Hearts touch in the fullness of the season
Growing, bearing fruit waiting for the harvest.

6

The indigo smoked glass is broken
The star fishes swim in the sea of the night sky
The bushes are outlined against the fading light
And a lonely coyote howls his homage to the moon
Once again we meet in the harbor of the night
In the warm mushy arms of the mother
Mother to all who are in-tune to the music of life
We beat our chest and bellow with the exaltation of life.

7

At the top of the high rocks the piper sang as the lights danced through
    the night
The piercing tones swirled around her head
As the day's cares fall away, she is free
As free as the birds that fly through the sky
Free as the water falling down the mountainside
Free to float on the color of sound
Sounds of peace, joy and happiness with mother earth.

8

I am not my body, I am spirit, I am free
The music of my soul inspires and releases me
To turn once again to the answers within
The rose petals fall off one by one until the bud of self remains
Pink and yellow fantasies await my delight there
The spirit guides us, gliding through the waves of the universe always
    one, yet always
separate
The mystery only music can express
and is revealed to us as truth

Linda Frank
Hethalyn Godwin
Ann Yates
Pat Sampson
Betty Giardini
Sue Barbara
Ingrid Baris
Nancy Liston

Welcome Home

Lynne Zielinski
Huntsville, Alabama

I am not... to paraphrase the Elephant Man... a Yankee. I am a Southerner. Transplanted here over twenty years ago from the northern hinterlands, I have, by osmosis and careful study, become a hard-core southern woman. Damn me if you will, but in the great tradition of Scarlett, "I'll nevah go north again."

Southern hospitality envelops me. Shop keepers, with their, "Y'all come back," invite me to return, whether I spend a dime or a dollar. No longer do I have to endure the glare of a clerk ready to close for the night, with his, "Oh, geeze, Charlie, I told ya ta lock the door. Okay, whatta youse guys want." Meeting the eyes of a stranger up north could get you killed. Here, you get a smile.

Friendships, not easily forged in Yankeeland, are readily available and everyone calls me, "Hon."

For all you new arrivals, I have a few little tips:

Weather: Don't laugh during your first winter down south. At first, I also wore sweaters and scoffed at the slight nip in the air and at my neighbors all bundled up in coats and scarfs and mittens and caps. Excuse me; I mean toboggans. Northerners slide down snow-covered hills on toboggans. Here, you wear them on your head; it's a language thing. Bit by bit, layer by layer, you'll gradually add a coat, a hat until — Voila! Twenty degree weather will be — to you, too — the Alaskan tundra.

Your first summer may take some adjustment. Beware of your first venture out under southern summer skies. Up north, it may take you from April through August to achieve a nice pale shade of cream-laden coffee. In the land of Dixie, two hours in our sun will find you shivering under a velour blanket, screeching skin aflame with pain.

That first summer I found it was too hot to garden in the yard. Happily, I can now go out in the yard and rearrange rocks in any weather. Although, unlike Miss Ava Gardner who, according to Orson Welles, "Never perspires, she glows," I pass perspire and go flat out to sweat — like

56   *Ordinary and Sacred As Blood*

a hog-tied hound (notice my attempts to familiarize you with the native vernacular). I so much admire the little Alabama ladies, out in their yards with pretty sunbonnets and flowered gardening gloves, not a trace of moisture or dirt on their lovely skin.

Travel: Beware of drivers who zip past in right or left lanes; it's legal but scary. Slower drivers prefer to amble along in the left lane and seem to enjoy the convoy-feel of tail-gaters. You needn't be on the lookout for turn signals; the folks have usually made their turn before signaling — so, keep your brakes in top shape. Ladies, don't bother to try and charm the policeman or deputy who stops you. Southern women have made the officers impervious to our paltry charms. And, be sure to wave back at those waving at you; they're just friends you haven't yet met.

Food: Those of you with cholesterol problems should approach the home-made southern biscuit with caution, if at all. Light as a feather, these temptresses are loaded with lard and will clog up your leaders (southern medical term for artery/vein) in a New York minute. When hosting a dinner party, never serve your veggies al dente. Green beans, corn, carrots and squash must simmer for hours — until pale (veggies, not host). If no ham hock is added to the simmering pot, the host must, as a good neighbor, slap on slabs of thick butter before serving.

Most of all, from the mountains of Fort Payne to the white sands of Gulf Shores, relax and enjoy our ever-present cotton fields, friendly farmers and the easier pace. If you're just drifting through; y'all come back. If you're here to stay... Welcome Home.

Naola Beauty Academy, New Orleans, 1945

Natasha Trethewey
Auburn, Alabama

Made hair? The girls here
put a press on your head
last two weeks. No naps.

They learning. See the basins?
This where we wash. Yeah,
it's hot. July jam.

Stove always on. Keep the combs
hot. Lee and Ida bumping hair
right now. Best two.

Ida got a natural touch.
Don't burn nobody.
Her own's a righteous mass.

Lee, now she used to sew.
Her fingers steady
from them tiny needles.

She can fix some bad hair.
Look how she lay them waves.
Light, slight and polite.

Not a one out of place.

Beauty Shop

Helen Blackshear
Montgomery, Alabama

This is a place for women growing old,
Where operators with a practiced smile
And skillful hands will improvise a style
To show off thinning hair that once was gold.
Rheumatic joints may rest from winter's cold,
Bent backs take respite for a little while
Where there are wrinkle creams and nails to file
And friendly talk while silver curls are rolled.

Smooth young faces seldom visit here.
The young with supple limbs and windblown hair
Rush out at life and have no time to spare
For aging ones like these who live with fear
Yet deck themselves in gallant finery,
Each with her dream of how she used to be.

Broken Toasters and Burnt Toast

Linda Strange
Huntsville, Alabama

When I got married, I received four toasters. I planned to take three back to the department store and keep one, but my Dad asked me to please give Mom one. So I did.

The toaster I kept lasted one year. It burnt up all my toast for a couple of months, then was more or less on its last leg for about eight months, then it finally went kaput.

Over thirty years of marriage, I have owned ten toasters. That's one every three years. A better record than that first toaster, but still not good. My last toaster worked well for two and a half years. I was hoping it would outlive the previous eight, but the last six months of its life, it burned everything.

It would pop down fine, but it wouldn't pop back up. I'd get busy putting breakfast on and the next thing I knew, smoke would come billowing forth. My husband said he always knew when breakfast was ready because the smoke alarm would go off!

Anyway, that was number nine. I was so aggravated I decided to just cook all my toast in the oven broiler. I soon found out you can burn toast a whole lot faster under the broiler than in the toaster.

So last year, my husband asked his Mom to get me a toaster like hers. For Christmas, she gave me this nice, expensive toaster with two large slots big enough for English muffins. I went out and got some nice, big raisin covered English muffins.

One Sunday morning as I was rushing around getting ready for church, I placed the muffins in the two large slots. Knowing that since this was a brand new toaster, and surely it would pop up by itself, I went about preparing breakfast. You guessed it. Soon I smelled smoke and our smoke alarm went off.

As smoke poured out of the toaster, my husband said the muffins I bought were too big and they were both jammed down in the thing, burning to charcoal. He stuck a FORK inside the toaster to dislodge them. At this

Ordinary and Sacred As Blood

point sparks flew, and not just from me. The thing was still plugged in! It made a few fizzing noises, dislodged the now charred muffins and went on to toaster heaven with the other nine. We ate burnt English muffins that morning and were late to church.

By now you have probably guessed the moral to this distasteful tale. The toaster I gave Mom thirty years ago still works. Every time I see it in their house, I get aggravated all over again. I don't know whether to be mad at Dad for making me give it to Mom. Or mad at her for taking such good care of it that it's lasted thirty years. Or mad at that ONE toaster that decided to be the ONLY one out of the four to last that long.

I've often wondered what happened to the other two that I took back to the store. For all I know, they may still be sitting in some little housewife's kitchen, peacefully doing their job RIGHT after all these years. I just don't want to know about it!

Matrushka Doll

Mary Carol Moran
LaFayette, Alabama

The outermost doll
Lives ebulliently,
Loves with abandon.
I am seldom her.

The second doll
Is patient
And kind and takes
Good care of her children.

The third doll
Works hard
And takes responsibility.
She doesn't let people down.

The fourth doll
Tries to please everyone
And wonders sometimes
Who she is.

The fifth doll
Obeys forgotten commands
From never reliable
Voices of childhood unwisdom.

The sixth doll
Sleeps or
Sits and can't do
Much.

The seventh doll
can't breathe there's
no
air.

Common Song

Anne Markham Bailey
Birmingham, Alabama

I drink beer. I daydream. I fold clothes. I wash my pussy. I fold my
blankets. I unfold them. I drink water. I wonder what next. I answer
sometimes. I fix my hair. I sing a song. I drive the truck. I use the
telephone. I drop something off. I pick something up. I come home.
I come home. I sit on the porch. I lie on the bed. I read a book. I
play a scenario. I talk on the telephone. I almost cry. I do not cry. I
choke up is big enough. I think you can ruffle my feathers. I am right.
I drink beer. I daydream. I fold clothes. I wash my pussy.

Mathematician

Ora Dark
Auburn, Alabama

In all my hours of drudgery in school, the class that I felt would do me the least amount of good was math. It seemed to me that anything past addition and subtraction would be totally useless when I became a wife and mother. However, I have been proven wrong many times; math can be applied to nearly every situation.

Theory of Bathroom Proximity

The urgency with which you have to go to the bathroom when you are shopping increases in direct proportion to the proximity to the toilet. The severity of the distress you feel closest to the bowl is multiplied by two for each item carried, child with you, undergarment being removed, and for each inch the stall is under standard size. Square that sum if you are wearing a jumpsuit that buttons down the front. Odds are you won't make it if you have any of the following factors working against you:

1. a long line outside the restroom,
2. a sign out front saying that the restroom is closed,
3. a child who has to go before you,
4. a bladder that is 40 years old, or
5. an urge to laugh, cough, or sneeze.

Work out the math before you have to go.

The Positive Power of Negative Spending

The flow of money into my checkbook is less than the flow of money out of the checkbook, therefore creating a minus money situation. Minus money has no denomination. It is produced by credit cards and checks from thin air, unless you are with the government.

The moment you think you have the maximum amount, your favorite department store will have a huge clearance sale, on stuff you needed to buy anyway, for 50 to 75 percent off the sale price. But even though you are saving loads of money, it's still minus money, and the two minuses do not add up to a plus. If you have more minus money than anyone you know, are you rich?

"Deadly Embrace" is the accounting term used to describe what happens when too many people try to get money out at one time. I think it sounds romantic, and it's happening to my checkbook more often than it happens to me. My checkbook could be considered great romantic fiction.

The Internal Escalation of Debt to Love Ratios

If you buy your daughter, Suzy, a candy bar at the supermarket, then your son, Tommy, gets to go to the movies. Therefore, Suzy gets to have a friend spend the night, which automatically means that Tommy gets $50 to go to Six Flags with his friend. Naturally, Suzy gets to go to cheerleading camp to the tune of about $250 and the offended Tommy will certainly have to have a stereo in his room to ease the pain.

But, if you really want to be fair, Suzy should have a TV/VCR in her bedroom, and Tommy will then want his own car. This whole equation means absolutely nothing if you really don't love them anyway, or never loved him or her as much as the other one. Financing? See minus money.

Axioms of Aggravation

1. If your gas tank is on empty, why does the only gas station close enough to rescue you have the most expensive gas prices in town? And the dirtiest restroom?

2. If you bring in 2 bags of groceries, for which you pay more than $30, why do you only get one meal and take out 4 bags of trash?

3. If you only ate 650 calories today, why did you gain 2 pounds?

4. If you pay $200 for a doctor's visit, buy 3 prescriptions for $58, and wait 2 hours in the waiting room, why don't you feel better?

5. If you just saved your husband $500 on furniture, why is he banging his head on the floor?

Mrs. Murphy Melancholy

Susan Murphy
Birmingham, AL

It hit me in the aisles of Walmart. For the first time in fifteen years, I had no reason to buy scented markers, no excuse for throwing happy face stickers into my cart. There were no giant letters to cut out, no macaroni noodles to dye, nothing whatsoever to laminate. For me, construction paper was a thing of the past.

You see, this fall there will be no Mrs. Murphy, Room 101. The new crop of kindergartners will be bringing their knock-knock jokes and skinned knees to another teacher. After a lot of soul searching, I decided to trade in my crayons for a word processor, leave teaching, at least for a while, and try writing full time. Time is marching on. At this point in my life, I've got to fish or cut bait, as my Dad would say, so I decided to set *One Fish, Two Fish, Red Fish, Blue Fish* aside for a while and turn my full attention to baiting publishers. From now on, if someone calls me Mrs. Murphy, they'll be trying to sell me something.

Leaving Mrs. Murphy behind isn't as easy as I thought it would be. Back in May, when all of the crayons were broken and I was bone tired, I gladly packed up my files and went home. Now, standing amidst the back-to-school stacks of colored pencils and three ring binders, I find myself going through teacher withdrawal.

There were warning signs all summer, of course. I couldn't bring myself to throw away egg cartons or toilet paper rolls. My garage is still full of milk jugs and shoeboxes, and I hauled home yet another refrigerator box because I knew it could be turned into a dandy playhouse. These urges will pass with time, I'm sure, but right now, I'm stuck in arts and crafts limbo.

But that's not the real problem. I'm having a hard time dealing with the fact that there will be no children for me to read to this year, no one to sing with. When you do grown up work at home, there are very few occasions that call for puppets, either, so I guess poor Mrs. Mooley and Burton the Brown Bear will be retiring as well. I'll have no one to play with. I will miss the loose teeth, the birthday cupcakes, and those magic moments when the letters begin to form words and take on meaning.

Ordinary and Sacred As Blood

On the social side of things, there will be no teachers' lounge to retreat to, no blessed inner sanctum where I can lick my wounds and prepare for my next project. I'll have no built in support group, no one to kvetch with over slices of chocolate cake sent in by some saintly parent.

I'll need to gather a new support group, I suppose, along with some new clothes. While writing at home doesn't have a dress code, there are only so many places a non-teacher can get away with wearing a kitty cat vest and a plastic necklace that meows. Right now, my closet contains nothing but "teacher clothes," which are different from civilian clothes in that they are comfortable, sensible and cute to the point of being nauseating to anyone over eight years old.

Jumpers are the backbone of a good kindergarten teacher's wardrobe. There's a reason for this, of course. It's hard to participate in a rousing game of "Duck, Duck, Goose" in a silk suit and five inch heels. Jumpers are loose fitting, letting your body relax so your mind can concentrate on the important things, like lunch money and whose turn it is to lead the Pledge of Allegiance. Serious teacher jumpers are also of the "no great loss" variety. If you wander into the path of some wayward fingerpaint or flying Spaghettios, you have to be ready to send your outfit, without fanfare, to the Great Goodwill Beyond. If you wore designer labels in the classroom, you'd be tempted to forego that paper mache piñata project or planting tulip bulbs outside the classroom window. Silk jumpers? That would be just plain silly.

I know I've made the right decision. It's going to be a good year, just different. Sooner or later, I'll shake this Mrs. Murphy melancholy and move on to the work at hand. Still, it wouldn't hurt to pick up just one package of stickers in case I get discouraged at some point. Even rejection slips must look better with happy faces on them.

My Sisters

Linda Frank
Huntsville, Alabama

I was always glad not to have a sister. That was before, when I thought having a sister meant having less. Less space of my own, less of Mom and Dad's attention. It might've even meant sharing clothes and toys that I didn't want to share and who knows what else.

Now it feels different. Having sisters means sharing myself, parts of me that I couldn't trust to show to anyone, couldn't risk being me, and being accepted.

It's taken time but now I have eight sisters, not by blood, but by choice.
They are all different, they are all special.
I have risked letting them see me... the real me.
They have heard me and accepted me as I am.

We have shared ourselves and many experiences along the way, our pain, our joy, our struggles and we have cried.
They have changed me these women that I now call sisters.

Ordinary and Sacred As Blood

Poet

Mary Carol Moran
LaFayette, AL

Catch
      a fly
with chopsticks
Click

Pin an
      emotion
to the
page

Final Examination

Dorothy Diemer Hendry
Huntsville, Alabama

Teachers from various schools of the city and county filed into the examination room. Although they themselves had given many a test, they took their seats with more anxiety than their students had ever felt. "Will we pass? Will we graduate?" they asked one another.

They knew they could not avoid the examination. They had been summoned from classrooms and offices, from vacation cottages and cruise ships, from libraries and churches, and even from loving hands that tried to hold them fast. To keep their appointment in this room, they had traveled on a road as cold as an operating table and as forlorn as the howling demons of Hell.

In the examination room the teachers felt warm at last, but they could not ease their weary bodies on the hard chairs. Why were the walls bare? What lay beyond the mysterious door opposite the entrance?

Since the teachers had come empty-handed, they waited for a Proctor to bring test booklets and pencils; and while they waited, they talked together anxiously.

"I don't know enough!" cried one teacher. "I studied all my life, but I could only show my students how to learn."

"Sometimes I didn't teach," confessed another. "If a child needed food or a warm coat or words of encouragement, I cared for that child first."

A third teacher sighed. "I tried to bring out the best in my students, but I often failed. Then I had to devise other methods and try again."

A fourth teacher shook his head. "People told me I should use my talents to become rich or famous or powerful, but the problems of school administration demanded all the talents I had."

A fifth teacher groaned. "I lost my teaching position when I campaigned for school tax reform."

The oldest teacher laughed aloud. The others stared at her. She said, "You ought to see your faces — all droopy and woebegone. Don't you remember how good you felt when you laughed with your students?"

"You're right!" a man answered. "We had to have a sense of humor."

All the teachers began to smile at each other and to tell stories of their teaching days.

"My students and I liked to make our classroom look interesting and attractive. I called them my budding scientists and artists."

"Remember the brightness of those young faces?"

"Remember the excitement of discovering something new together?"

"The clever ones and the slower ones and the bold and the shy — they all needed me."

"Yes, and we helped them realize they needed each other, too."

"How did we ever manage so many enterprises? Field trips, science fairs, math contests, spelling bees, literary magazines, pep rallies, games, concerts, plays, Halloween carnivals, Thanksgiving parades, assemblies, and proms: something for everyone so that everyone could shine."

"Remember how they looked in their caps and gowns — so terribly young and vulnerable? We wondered if we had taught them enough."

"When we met them years later, we hardly recognized them: they looked so mature and responsible. But they greeted us fondly, and we felt immensely proud of them."

"It was great to be a teacher! I would do it all over again!"

The teachers' voices and laughter rose in crescendo. At the very height of their merriment, the mysterious door swung open. The teachers fell silent. They had almost forgotten the examination. Would it be too difficult? Would they fail?

A tall, stern-looking Proctor strode though the doorway into the room. The teachers perceived that behind him unfurled vistas of fields and woods and gardens and alabaster cities with houses and schools and people working and singing together and children running and playing in the sunlight. The teachers felt a warm breeze caress their bodies with healing and fragrance and joy.

"You have already had your examination," said the Proctor, "and all of you have passed."

His voice was rich and musical, and he smiled the most loving smile they had ever seen.

"Teachers, we need you here. Welcome!"

Tribute

Judy Ritter
Gadsden, Alabama

I heard your name read today:
A solemn note echoing off stony faces
    and mingling with lingering wails of pipes.
I saw your son step slowly through the crowd
    and spread his hands to receive your tributes:
Your nation's flag of red, white, and blue
    and a rose of red offered from a symbolic vase.
I listened as an instrument of your work — a C 130 — roared overhead
    against vast autumn skies of blue
    and as a lone fire siren shrilled in the distance:
A call piercing the day with poignant finality.
I wept as men and women touted the praises
    of "the 94" with stories of bravery and dedication
    and promises of eternal remembrance.
I read the bronze plaque to be planted forever around a Maltese Cross
    and traced my fingers across the letters of your name:
My brief moment of pride and private salute.
And finally, as scores of uniformed men and women
    ended their cadenced walk
    and ceremony turned into ordinary,
I released the pull,
I broke the string,
    and joyfully,
I felt your spirit soar!

*Written for my sister-in-law who was honored as a
"Fallen Firefighter" at the national monument.*

Ordinary and Sacred As Blood

Raising Children

White Lies

Natasha Trethewey
Auburn, Alabama

The lies I could tell,
when I was growing up
light-bright, near-white,
high-yellow, red-boned
in a black place,
were just white lies.

I could easily tell the white folks
that we lived uptown,
not in that pink and green
shanty-fied shot-gun section
along the tracks. I could act
like my homemade dresses
came straight out the window
of Maison Blanche. I could even
keep quiet, quiet as kept,
like the time a white girl said
(squeezing my hand) *now
we have three of us in this class.*

But I paid for it every time
Mama found out.
She laid her hands on me,
then washed out my mouth
with Ivory soap. *This
is to purify,* she said,
and cleanse your lying tongue.
Believing her, I swallowed suds
thinking they'd work
from the inside out.

Special Birth

Janet SJ Anderson
Huntsville, Alabama

Out from the rake of shadow,
From these brawn elm-bone rafters;
Braces for my house,
A spined-leaf child's
Green stick bone
Sprouts.
Branches out,
Fragile from my own,
Belly into ground,
Growing,
Fingering into crevices,
Blossoming,
Like flowers into stone.

Stretching An Athletic Supporter

Ora Dark
Auburn, Alabama

Do I look like an Athletic Supporter? I'm only one of thousands of devoted followers of assorted sport seasons. Let's take a little inventory to find the net value of a mom with athletes in elementary school. We begin with sign-up for soccer in the fall, basketball in the winter, and then more soccer or baseball for spring. Here is a highly technical equation for those who are analytical.

If your child is in sports, here is how it adds up:

Multiply: the number of children in sports

times the number of sports your child is in

times the number of children you must supervise or carpool for each game or practice.

Square: the above sum if your husband is a coach or assistant coach.

Add: **One point** for every uniform item you must purchase per player, for each piece of equipment you purchase per sport, for washing the uniform for each game, for knowing the name of the team, the name of the coach, or if your child's team won.

Two points for each time you had to bring snacks or drinks for the players, knew any of the rules, showed up for the team picture, knew where the game was being played, and cheered for a great play no matter who it was.

Five points for making dinner on a practice or game night, knowing what position your child is playing, taking pictures of your child getting her trophy, or going to the team party.

Ten points for being team mother, making out the drinks roster, planning the team party, or having concession duty in 90 degree weather.

Random points will be given on a discretionary basis for staying awake, for talking to the other moms while still keeping your child in view and for bringing umbrellas when it rains.

Subtract: **One point** for kissing your child or calling them a pet name in front of the other kids, not buying the exact shoe all the other kids have, mentioning how great an athlete your neighbor's kid is, crying when you get hit with the ball, or letting a sibling run on to the field during play.

Two points for talking to them at all in front of the team, offering a jacket to them if it's cold, being late for practice, or saying hello to the coach.

Five points for asking the coach how your child is doing, talking to another mom about you on any topic, or having the wrong kind of drinks for the team.

Ten points for tucking their shirt in, tying their shoes, or combing their hair at practice or the game, in front of the other team.

Twenty points for yelling at the coach, giving your own child directions during the game, forgetting your turn at the concession stand in 90 degree weather, or not making any effort to sell barbecue tickets or candy for the team.

Scoring:

0- 50 points
Some support is needed, perhaps eating out one night will help. A few hot showers and some TLC and you'll recover.

51 - 80 points
Sedation in the evenings, total bedrest on the weekends and a cruise couldn't hurt.

81 - 100 points
Summer camp for the kids, two weeks of solitary confinement with shock treatment and shots for that twitch you've developed. You may drool a little.

Over 100 points
Fake your own death; it starts again in September.

Introducing Girl

Kelly Magee
Auburn, Alabama

Blow out the candles and you're thirteen.
Your mother nods matronly, "Now you can
go." She holds your hand all the way to
the mall, and you aren't sure why, but she's
singing that song about the Animal's Fair,
"the big baboon is combing his hair,"
the one she sang when you were small and
scared of the man in your dreams. She calls you
"my girl" to the black-bibbed lady at the Sears'
make-up counter, but you're thirteen, and
you know you're a babe, a chick, a dame,
a honey, a fox, a full blown teenager, an almost
adult — in two years you'll be able to drive,
Christ's sake, and then you won't need her
or her song to escape the nighttime fears that
blow into your room of men without faces
who wait for you in your dreams.

You drop mother's hand as the make-up
technician tests your skin, and it's normal
(thank god), oil-free and water-resistant,
just enough pink and just enough yellow
to make you look real. Then, Behold, your
cheekbones, so high you could run away with
two thin-bearded men and eat grapes in a silver
convertible, like the girl in the poster over
your head whose lipstick has saved the day.
Now they're smearing red juicy gloss on your
lips and saying they'll reinvent your face, and you

wonder if after the creation is complete they'll
look at you and say: Just perfect! She's our
girl of the future, she defines our style, a new
kind of natural, easy to assemble in five matching
parts. She's 100% pure (with certain sexual
side effects), a true illusion, she's making it happen,
flawless, smooth, weightless, controlled, she'll
take your breath away. And then, to the man,
Lookee here, young lad, it's the girl of your dreams.

It's you that's in front when you leave, leading
your mother through smoke-smudged eyes, and now
the whole world is smoke-smudged eyes. Later
that night, your mom waves good-night from
the couch — she's known for some time you're
too big to tuck in — and it feels like something
is burrowing deep down in your chest. In your
dreams that night, the faceless man doesn't
look so frightening. In fact, you might want
to marry him some day. Wouldn't it be fun
and wouldn't you be so proud to ride in his
convertible? He steps out of your dream, and
you take his face; that is, you take nothing at all,
and when you look in the mirror you see
nothing at all. He takes you away to live at
the Animal's Fair, that colorful encampment
that is the place of your dreams.

Anna

Elsie Azar
Huntsville, Alabama

A long time ago, in a small industrial town in Pennsylvania — where large families were common and livable wages were rare — a factory worker delivered good news to little Anna's mother. Since Anna's father was blind and unable to earn a wage, the factory was offering her family the new job opening.

Anna, only 13, was the youngest of nine children and the only one who was not bringing a paycheck home. Knowing that she would have to take the job, she began to cry. She would have to quit school and forego her dream of having her own business one day. But as painful as it was, it was still better than having to take her father to local taverns every Saturday night begging, "Can you spare a few cents to help my blind father?"

When Anna's mother signed the necessary legal papers — permitting a minor to work at the factory — Anna's childhood was planned. She traded her school books and tablet for a black lunch box, and the following day she walked to her job at the Pittsburgh Plate Glass Company.

During the following year at PPG, Anna made many friends, most of whom thought she was older, 15 or 16, which made her feel grown up. She never told them about her greatest fear. Twelve-foot high sheets of glass were stored on large racks near her work area. Secured in an upright position, slightly tilted to keep them from toppling, they towered over Anna as a constant threat.

One day while she was at her work station, she heard a crackling sound coming from above. She looked upward through the tall glass panels in time to see the ceiling rafters collapse. Pieces of rotted wood, metal and asbestos began to fall. Chunks of debris ripped away from the ceiling and hammered at the vulnerable 12 foot sheets. As the panels exploded, pieces of broken glass and slivers thrust in all directions. There was no place, no time, to run. Anna suddenly became the little girl she had left behind a year ago. Her pupils dilated, her eyes transfixed with horror, and her body rigid. Although the sound of breaking glass is easily dismissed in a glass plant, this one signaled "danger". By the time it stopped, the entire floor of workers stood before her in awe.

Glass fragments surrounded Anna while large pieces of broken glass hung suspended over her head, virtually encasing her. The slightest move would have caused them to crash into her body, resulting in fatal injuries. She was paralyzed with fear. While department heads and foremen argued about the best way to free her, one of the workers, a young woman, came forward, ready to lay her own safety on the line.

"Build me some scaffolding. Different levels," she said, looking up at the remaining ceiling that could fall any minute. "I'll have to start at the top and lift each piece away, one by one." While the men quickly started to assemble the scaffolds, she reassured Anna. "Don't be afraid, kid. I have the best hands in this place. You'll live to grow up and name your first daughter after me."

After the scaffolds were in place, the workers gathered in silent prayer, watching. The Good Samaritan removed each lethal piece of glass with the precision of a surgeon until Anna was out of danger. When it was over, the crowd cheered and applauded while Anna and her hero hugged each other and cried.

****

Every Christmas as I was growing up, my mother would tell me this story. Then she would start her annual card and note to the woman she could never forget. With little variation, she would write:

> Dear Elsie,
> I think of you often. My grocery store business is good, better than my arithmetic. But my banker says I count my money just fine. Ha.Ha.
> As always, my daughter Elsie says hello.
> Your devoted friend, Anna

A Mother To Her Young

Laura Hunter
Northport, Alabama

children

i stood naked
my body moist with dew
the morning nature held her balance
and you were ripped from my belly

howling

children

i stand naked
my body now shriveled and dry
as nature tips her scale
and lifts my throat taut for your scalpel

stinging

i remember the prick from the eve within
i know still the burn of the serpent's strike
i watch you talk round me as if i were a chair
preparing me for what you do not know I have always known

the moment life begins death is

dawning

we sit naked

waiting

Even Sweetly Scattered

Helen Norris
Montgomery, Alabama

Little girls together are always in a circle
Even when they aren't.
Even sweetly scattered
Swinging from the willows, swimming in the grass
Pressing their faces into green ground moss
Storing blue feathers in the pocket of a sweater
Even sweetly scattered
In a deep down circle they are kneeling
In the circle of a sky-filled pool that
Holds the petaled cluster of their faces in the water
With thoughts that are woven of the same green thread
Gentling desires that are fawns of the morning
Damp with milkweed, thistledown to touch.

Their eyes are gray squirrels
Storing nuts for the winter.

To June, benevolent heart

Susan Luther
Huntsville, Alabama

My daughter is the light
of the summer sky, plucking

all the petals from wild daisy
to end on *he loves me not.*

He loves me: born
on the wind

after a night
when no wine

was necessary,
when eyes reached prayer

deep & praising fingers
held no line.

We danced as if
all the old songs

were our new songs,
here we are.

Here we are.
We fed each other

chocolate & cream
from the same ardent

silver, ripe tomatoes,
olives, all that spoons

the thrilling tongue. Moon-
struck   we did not even

make it home,
stopped the truck,

worshipped all the places
God is on the sunblessed desert

ground. If ever
there were a love-child

she is, you are
that woman:

of your father's dove-star
eyes, my parti-colored hair.

Big with grace, fair changes
now, you cannot

imagine any
of the lives the two

of us have dreamed
for you —

darling,
you dream your own.

The Mom Look

Susan Murphy
Birmingham, Alabama

As soon as the words were out of your mouth, you knew you had gone too far. Mom turned, assumed her most powerful stance, and fixed you with a gaze so deadly that you despaired of ever being able to speak again. the Mom Look.

Since the beginning of time, moms have been in charge of creating functioning social beings out of the natural chaos of childhood. Since this does not happen overnight, every day can become a litany of "chew with your mouth closed," "don't hit your sister," "put your napkin in your lap," "don't hit your sister."

Through years of disciplinary trial and error, the Mom Look developed, saving wear and tear on the maternal vocal chords, and giving intelligent children one last chance to avoid more direct physical intervention. (A side note: the Mom Look was perfected by my mother back in 1961, on the day that I told her I would come to the table when I was good and ready.)

Sadly, the ability to effectively deliver the Mom Look does not magically appear when you enter the maternity ward. It takes time to harness its power and develop your own particular style. (New moms, just practice in front of a mirror until you hit upon a look that makes you feel guilty, then lock and load.)

While there are many variations, for me, the Mom Look involves slowly crossing the arms, lowering the chin, and delivering a death ray stare that says, "Think again" in no uncertain terms. Properly executed, the Mom Look triggers the child's shame mechanism and causes an immediate improvement in behavior.

The beauty of the Mom Look is that it is wordless and can be executed in almost any situation without drawing peripheral attention. In social situations, however, like during church or at the dinner table with your sister-in-law's perfect family, you may have to use the Abbreviated Mom Look. Simply turn your head slowly and deliver a short but pointed stare.

Ordinary and Sacred As Blood

If you have been using the Full Mom Look for a while, your children will fill in the rest of the movements and get the message. If the infraction is serious, add a raised eyebrow. If you have to lift both eyebrows, your children should hear, "Just wait until we get home."

Of course, the Mom Look is powerless if your children won't look at you. In more constricted situations, I have tried the Svengali approach, attempting to get my children's attention by mental telepathy, but it never worked. Moms may have eyes in the back of their heads, but children do not. In fact, children can become completely oblivious whenever they want to, which is why they need maternal intervention in the first place.

Once my daughters go off to college, I won't have any idea whether they are putting their napkins in their laps or not. They could forgo thank you notes altogether. It will be out of my hands. At that point, it will be time for us to establish an adult-to-adult relationship, where advice is given only when sought and my suggestions will be just ... suggestions.

Of course, once my daughters have children of their own, things will be different. During Thanksgiving dinner, when they are busy unleashing the power of their own Mom Looks over spilled gravy or a smart aleck comeback, I'm going to put on my newly developed Grandmother Look, and laugh, and laugh...

Farewell to a Teenager

Frances Cooper Smith
Montgomery, Alabama

Walk to the door with her, mother,
You must not kiss her goodbye,
She is no child any longer,
You cannot keep her, don't try.

Hurrying off to what waits her
Eager, she goes on her way,
Heedless of all you might tell her,
There is no word you can say.

Send out your love to protect her,
Peril is rife in the street,
Send out your thoughts to defend her,
Snares will entangle her feet.

There is a danger unreckoned,
There is a danger more real
Than heartbreak waiting to meet her
Than crashing of glass and steel.

Time has so altered her childhood
And time can estrange, as well,
Walk to the door with her, mother,
Wave as you bid her farewell.

Ordinary and Sacred As Blood

Short Childhood

Faye Gaston
Union Springs, Alabama

Your childhood's past.
It went too fast.
How could I know
How fast you'd grow?
Time will not wait
Or hesitate.
I watch confused.
The present moved.

Golden Trees

Ramey Channell
Leeds, Alabama

All through that passionate summer,
With our intemperate sun
Burning and beckoning,
Your face remained the face of a child,
Still dreaming dreams of childhood
As you played beneath summer trees.

Then, like changing leaves and seasons,
So quickly you became
What you had not been.
Climbing skyward into the mass of gold and red,
You left behind familiar earth and dreams
Seeking higher, newer things.

I watched the sudden change as you,
Bewitched by one cool breeze,
Balanced in a world
I had forgotten many autumns before.
Now, with your new cool and careless face before me,
I am haunted by memories of golden trees.

Kinfolk

Naming

Natasha Trethewey
Auburn, Alabama

August 1911

I cannot now remember the first word
I learned to write — perhaps it was my name,
Ophelia, in tentative strokes, a banner
slanting across my tablet at school, or inside
the cover of some treasured book. Leaving
my home today, I feel even more the need
for some new words to mark this journey,
like the naming of a child — *Queen, Lovely,*
Hope — marking even the humblest beginnings
in the shanties. My own name was a chant
over the washboard, a song to guide me
into sleep. Once, my mother pushed me toward
a white man in our front room. *Your father,*
she whispered. *He's the one that named you, girl.*

excerpt from "Storyville Diary"

Ordinary and Sacred As Blood

The Aunt's Tale

Rusty Bynum
Huntsville, Alabama

My aunt is small and spare, lean in a leathery way that fits just right with her coal black hair and intense dark eyes. That's why her voice is such a surprise, a round honeydew voice. She is my mother's only sister, more mother to me than aunt in these twenty years since my mother died. She's the keeper of the stories now, a job for which her sweet, full voice is perfectly suited.

Muton was set on taking his three daughters out in the boat; there wasn't a thing Macon could do to change his mind about that. It scared her to death, the very thought of having her girls on the water. Muton asked Macon to come in the boat, too, of course, hoping that she would even though he knew she wouldn't. She was terrified of water, couldn't swim a stroke.

"No," she said, "I'll just sit here on the shore and wait with Jean."

"You'll miss seeing the look on their faces when they feel the boat move," he said, but Macon shook her head and told him if he kept the boat close to shore she'd see them. He nodded okay and kissed her. She seemed to feel better 'til Muton whistled for Denny. I had to admit that old bird dog was graceful when he jumped in the boat, but Macon was mad as hops. She wheeled around and walked up the shore, muttering.

"It's a fine how-do-you-do when a man replaces his wife with a damned dog." Macon was so mad she didn't even stay to give the girls a kiss before they got in the boat. She plopped herself down in the sand and kept on fuming. I sat by her, patting her on the back, but I didn't say anything. I may have been her sister and her best friend, but even I couldn't say one word against Muton unless I wanted a tongue-lashing, which I didn't.

We sat on the shore together, burying our feet in the sand and watching the old rowboat rock Macon's family just out of reach of both of us. (I couldn't swim any more than Macon could.) We could see the girls, though, their sweet faces full of surprise and delight. Priscilla, the oldest, was sitting up front with Muton. Amelia and Louise, sitting in back, decided they wanted to face the other direction, see where they'd been instead of where they were going.

Macon and I heard Muton's voice stern and loud, "No!" Muton never shouted at his daughters, but this time he was mighty definite. "Both of you be STILL!"

It was too late, though; those girls were wobbling and twisting. Muton stood up to grab hold of their little shoulders and steady them, but when he did, Priscilla got scared and stood up to grab hold of her daddy. In less than a second, the whole bunch was in the water.

Muton came up first, his eyes wild and terrified, frantic. All three girls bobbed up about the same time, but they didn't stay up long. They were screaming and crying and gulping water with every breath. They'd flail their spindly arms and then disappear again, but that was enough for Muton to get a fix on them. Soon as he'd see one little head pop up, he was right there, taking hold. But he could only hold two. Macon and I saw that awful reality in his eyes, the terrible knowledge that two arms couldn't save three drowning babies. For one eternal second he resisted his burden of judgment, but we heard the sob that broke from his twisted face as he reached for Priscilla first, then Amelia, then turned away to drag them to the boat.

I grabbed hold of Macon before she could run into the lake. It was all I could do to hold her back, the terror made her so strong. I kept saying to her, over and over, "It won't help for you to drown, too." Finally, Macon stood on the shore, screaming and screaming, tearing at her clothes, at her hair, at the air, tearing at God Himself. And then she stopped, and smiled. Knowing she'd gone mad, I turned my eyes away, back to the boat with Priscilla and Amelia huddling together, crying, and Muton staring wild-eyed at the water, mouth agape, arms yearning and outstretched.

It was Denny he reached toward, that mangy, graceful, blessed bird dog, holding Louise by the shirt collar.

My aunt smiled, remembering. Then she sobered and her eyes turned darker than I'd ever seen them. "I promised them I'd never tell," she whispered. "They didn't want you to know. They were afraid you'd think you mattered less, think he loved you less to leave you in the water and take the other two." A tear rolled out. "But they're dead twenty years."

Her eyes were black holes in time — dark pools that swirled, pulled, held me prisoner. At last a small, strangled cry cracked the air between us.

"You're a grown woman now. You're old enough to understand it. Aren't you?"

Fix it, Pah-Pah

Van Potter
Phenix City, Alabama

Next door, Garner Lee, the deputy sheriff,
again had beaten Doll, his wife - my nursemaid,
who fried my bacon just right
and took me to pick blackberries in the woods.
Pah-Pah, your loaded shotgun
was where a five-year-old could reach it:
on the floor, between the wall
and the cherry oak headboard you carved.
So I dragged it out

by the trigger, snuggled it under my arm
and pulled it past the rocking chair that you'd made for me
and out the door and down
the 10 new, wooden steps you'd put up. I bounced
the butt until I reached the moist back yard.
I strained with it past my bike,
that, after your paint job, shined
red even in the shade of the giant mulberry tree.
At first you didn't see

me as you loomed under the wooden shelter
behind Chicken Comer's
where you barbecued boneless pork butts over a deep pit,
stirred up your special sauce
and got ready for your customers.

I grunted as I lifted the shotgun
to you: "Pah-Pah, shoot
Garner Lee!" and I repeated Doll's cry, "I'm tired
of his damn shit!" You snatched

up the shotgun. When I saw it two days later,
it was locked behind the glass door
of the wooden case you'd built high
on the wall over the mantel.
The bullets were boxed and at the back
of the top shelf of the china cabinet.
That same day, Garner Lee drove off with
his suitcases, and Doll made me
a blackberry pie.

Sticky-Wrapper Moms

Alma V. Sanders
Huntsville, Alabama

the other day
my daughter and her
daughter and I were
in my car coming home
from a junk-food outing

my granddaughter had
a sticky wrapper from
a McDonald's apple pie
and didn't know what
to do with it

so she gave that
sticky wrapper to
her mother who gave
it to her mother
who didn't have a
mother to give it
to   so she just
tossed it to the
back seat of her
car and said
"Oh, well."

Oh, Well!

Junk Man Dad

Mary Halliburton
Hope Hull, Alabama

"They're collectibles, for sure."
A brown bear with one eye, a glass rooster,
and a portrait of John Wayne painted on velvet,
pulled from the trunk of a car with no back seat.
"I got them all for two bucks."

He looks the world like Santa
with long white hair and beard,
old clothes, dusty shoes, a round belly,
the smell of sweat, his trademark.

He smiles, gives a gleeful laugh
and hands me a brown paper bag.
"This is the best. The reason I came down."

Wrapped in newsprint, the small
ceramic tiger and cub couldn't
be worth more than a dollar.
"Thanks, it's neat Dad," I say.
"Did you spend your lunch money?"

He shuffles his feet, grins.
"Bought a foot-long, day-old
sandwich for a dollar."

"You need vegetables."

"The sandwich had lettuce and tomato,
and look here... got this for two bucks."
He plucks a grocery bag from inside the car.

"Okra? Dad, it's not worth fifty cents."

"That's okay. The old man needed the money."

A Picture for Baba

Nabella Shunnarah
Birmingham, Alabama

A father's face is a sad thing to forget. My memories of good times with my father are filled with his smiling eyes, loving embraces and the aroma of his pipe tobacco. But unlike me, my father grew up without memories of a father.

Baba, as I called my father, would weep when he talked about growing up without a strong, nurturing male in his life. His father left the old country when Baba was small and Baba consoled himself by speaking of our grandfather constantly, telling us, his four children, to keep searching for any clue as to the whereabouts of our grandfather. Forty years of searching done by other relatives yielded only a little information: my grandfather, Foteh Salama, had gone to Chile and had died there sometime in the 1920s.

"Just a picture," Baba would wail. "If I could only find a picture of him... to see what he looked like."

For Palestinian families, roots are crucially important. Our genealogy was mapped out for us long ago and can be found in a book larger than the history of western civilization. Our family tree has deep roots stretching back more than 500 years and is documented in *The History of Ramallah*. Baba tore our family's page out and kept it in his small, dog-eared Arabic Bible. Our grandfather's name was on the tree, but what became of him when he left Ramallah was a mystery.

This is Baba's story:

Grandfather Foteh's four brothers and a nephew had traveled to South America, following their dreams of wealth and prosperity in the new world. They found work and sent money home but did not return themselves. Eventually, my grandfather volunteered to make the journey to Chile and bring back his brothers, but neither he nor they ever returned to Ramallah.

Each Arab son carries the name of his father as a middle name. Baba's name, Farah Foteh Salama, was one of which he was proud. Farah means joy, celebration; Salama comes from the word salaam which means peace.

Coming from a largely uneducated family with little resources, Baba, as a young man, also elected to go to America to work and support his now widowed mother and older brother. He soon discovered that the magic of money materialized only from hard work. He became a successful peddler of household goods to outlying country folks. With his tote of dry goods in his arm, Baba cheerily sold bedspreads, tablecloths, rugs and tapestries to country women with little access to urban shopping centers.

After many years, he returned to the old country to marry. Bringing home bolts of silky fabric, lace tablecloths and much needed cash, Baba returned to Ramallah in 1947 laden with my mother's trousseau. A modest wedding was prepared for him and my mother. He remained long enough to witness my birth in '48, then left us to return to his new business, a restaurant called The Bean House in Louisville, Kentucky. He promised to send for us as soon as financially possible.

That day came in September, 1953. My mother and I boarded a silver jet which brought us to the States, leaving behind my grandparents, an uncle, an aunt and my mother's sweet-smelling rose and tulip garden. Nostalgic immigrant stories attest to the pain of leaving one's country forever. My pain — the loss of five adults who loved me — was assuaged by Baba, whom I met at the age of five.

My parents worked together and raised four children. Through the years, Baba never forgot his dream... to find a picture of his father. As we, his children grew older he reiterated his wish to us, but we felt inept in dealing with this dilemma.

I married in 1967 and moved to Birmingham, Alabama. Baba requested of me to keep searching... perhaps someone in Alabama has connections in Chile. Sadly, Baba passed away in 1979 without learning any information about his father.

One day, while having lunch with a friend, I heard about a fellow countryman from Birmingham who'd visited a friend in Santiago, Chile. He spoke of a large Palestinian community in Santiago. The Chilean friend was president of the Palestinian club. I felt shivers run down my spine. Somehow I knew. That must be where my grandfather and his brothers had lived, I thought to myself. It was worth a try.

I wrote to the president of the club in Santiago. I gave him Arabic names of my grandfather and his brothers, approximate dates of when they may have lived there, etc. Weeks went by... I don't know if I expected an answer.

One clear cold day in December, 1994, I received a letter in the mail from Santiago, Chile. My heart was in my throat as I ripped open the letter. Out fell pictures and a letter written in broken English...

Dear Nabella,

My name is Lionel Jorges Cura Ronseco and I am your cousin.....Picture number one is your grandfather, Foteh Cura Misle...

I had no control of the tears spilling down my face. I could barely see to finish the letter. Lionel gave us the gift we'd been waiting for: a picture of my grandfather. He even sent pictures of the mausoleum where he is buried. Lionel didn't know my grandfather, but he heard that Foteh lived in Santiago for a while before he became ill and died in the early 1920s.

I stared at the picture of Foteh, looking for some resemblance to my father, but there was none. Baba would have been amused to know that Grandfather Foteh looked like Baba's brother.

I was amazed to learn that Lionel had also been searching for us. He is part of our family now. I sent him the family tree and showed him where his name belonged. He sent pictures of his family, wife, daughter, his brother and their families. I introduced him to names of relatives in Ramallah where he wants to go make his own connections.

The chapter entitled Foteh Salama has finally come to a close. Why he had remained a mystery was finally clear: he had changed his name to reflect Hispanic customs. In Chile, the mother's last name is used instead of the father's. When Foteh Salama became Foteh Cura Misle, he was difficult to find — but the thread of kinship is a strong one, stretching across oceans and generations.

A strong cold wind blew the day I took a short trek to Resthaven Cemetery where Baba lies. In one hand I carried carnations, my father's favorite flower; in my other hand was the letter.

Baba ... we found a picture.

Choices

Reese Danley-Kilgo
Huntsville, Alabama

The lace is yellowed, faded
brown around the edges,
satin ribbons frayed from use, and time.
Babies don't wear bonnets now,
but once they did. This is the cap
my grandmother kept.
"I had to choose," she said.

Savanna, mother of my father, loved
the Alabama land, green hills, and trees.
She did not want to leave.
But when her restless husband looked
with longing to the West, and heard
the call of Texas, she knew she had to go,
and did. The wagons rolling slowly west
were hard on women. Babies died, mothers
dried their tears, left their hearts
in small mounds, moved on.

She chose the knitted woolen cap
to bury her baby in. The wind
blows cold across the plains.
She kept the bonnet made of lace
and satin ribbons, passed it on.
It is the one I treasure now.

Frayed lace bonnet for a frail baby,
buried by a Texas trail,
I think of you, and of my grandmother,
who had to choose
to go or be left behind,
who had to choose which cap
to bury her baby in, which cap to keep.

Flounder

Natasha Trethewey
Auburn, Alabama

Here, she said, put this on your head.
She handed me a hat.
You 'bout as white as your dad,
and you gone stay like that.

Aunt Sugar rolled her nylons down
around each bony ankle,
and I rolled down my white knee socks
letting my thin legs dangle,

circling them just above water
and silver backs of minnows
flitting here then there between
the sun spots and the shadows.

This is how you hold the pole
to cast the line out straight.
Now put that worm on your hook,
throw it out and wait.

She sat spitting tobacco juice
into a coffee cup.
Hunkered down when she felt the bite,
jerked the pole straight up

reeling and tugging hard at the fish
that wriggled and tried to fight back.
A flounder, she said, *and you can tell*
'cause one of its sides is black.

The other side is white, she said.
It landed with a thump.
I stood there watching that fish flip-flop,
switch sides with every jump.

Ordinary and Sacred As Blood

Portrait

Janet SJ Anderson
Huntsville, Alabama

You sit for hours.
They have already hired another woman
To smile like you.
Another woman
Whose cheekbones they will erase
And darken.
My father disappeared this way.
They rubbed the skin off his face.
His jaw washed away
In linseed and turpentine.
They made him sit for hours,
Flattening his fleshtones,
Tipping his head
Until his chin fell off.
Afraid daylight might come
And find them painting with their fingers:
Painters, who never saw us
The way we might be,
Who canvassed their brushes,
Who scraped and oiled us as they pleased.

Bridges Of Glass

Carolyn Buchanan
Auburn, Alabama

Bonnie and Para Lee were bitter bookends, volumes of loneliness and pride between them. The maiden Brock sisters were not true mirror images, but no one in our family ever spoke one name without the other. Bonnie-and-Para Lee. Canker and sore... rock and hard place... sour and puss.

Both women were diminutive in stature. Para Lee had a dainty, prissy air about her; her feline face registered self-satisfaction. Her slightly older sister Bonnie looked as if the soul inside her had shrunk a size, leaving the outside shell shriveled. The lines around her thin mouth had settled into a permanent frown. Their matching pale blue eyes were flinty and remote most of the time, a look I sometimes saw in their older brother, my Grandfather Macon. They were born old.

Bonnie lived alone, next door to my grandparents. When I was five years old, I would sneak over to her house. She would open the back door and silently let me into her kitchen when she noticed me waiting on the porch, peeking in. I watched as she cooked her solitary meal out of tiny pots. They looked like doll pans to me; I was fascinated by them. I can still smell the pungent odor of roast beef and vegetables which permeated her small duplex apartment. As I look back, I wonder if Bonnie really wanted a little shadow trailing after her. I wonder if she even noticed when I stopped coming a few years later. I like to think she missed me, at least a little bit. My visits had become an accepted habit.

I saw Para Lee mostly on holidays, when my father's family converged at my grandparents' house for dinner. She would drive up from her beloved Atlanta, and all my other aunts, uncles, and cousins would gather as well. While the adults gossiped and prepared the meal, the children would run upstairs to play hide-and-seek until summoned.

One Thanksgiving when I was ten, Para Lee collared me before I could make my escape with the others. After skeptically viewing my efforts at arranging flatware, she announced, "Carolyn, it's time you learned how to properly set a table."

Everyone knew that once Para Lee fastened her attention upon you, you might as well go along quietly with whatever she had in mind.

"Now, take these linen placemats, for example. One shouldn't simply position them haphazardly. Each should be neatly placed on the table," she intoned. She picked up an errant, starched white rectangle of cloth and rearranged it to her precise specifications. "The napkin should be folded symmetrically, placed with the crease to the inside of the plate."

I nodded morosely, not daring to speak or challenge her in any way. If I did, I'd be treated to an hour long lecture on the history of table linens, or something. Keeping my eyes fixed in front of me, I simply nodded.

"The placement of the silverware is extremely important," she droned on. "Forks to the left of the service plate— salad fork on the outside, dinner fork beside it. Knife and spoons on the right of the china — knife blade to the inside, of course." She placed all the sterling just so, and turned a smug face to mine. Reaching into her apron pocket, she withdrew a ruler. "Each utensil must be exactly one inch from the border of the mat."

She ceremoniously handed me the wooden stick as if it were a scepter. "Set the table as I've taught you, and I'll come and check everything when you're finished."

At that moment, ruler in hand, I felt like I didn't measure up. I had hoped trying to help would be enough to please her, but apparently it wasn't. Nothing ever was.

Four years ago, my mother called on the telephone.

"Para Lee is in the hospital. It's serious."

Dutifully, I made the journey back to my hometown to see her. Carrying a small bouquet of dyed pink carnations I had picked up at the grocery, I walked up to the Floyd Hospital information desk.

"I'm here to see Miss Para Lee Brock. I have flowers," I added stupidly. The nurse tediously checked the computer for her room number.

"She died this morning. Her room's already been assigned to someone else," she said. She didn't even bother to look up from the monitor.

I laid the flowers on the counter and left. Para Lee and I had missed each other once again.

Through Open Windows

Ruth Thomas Halbrooks
Birmingham, Alabama

If I could look through open windows now
And view nostalgic scenes of long ago,
The family sitting near the firelight's brow
And oil lamps burning with a mellow glow,
I would see Mama slowly rocking there,
Upon her lap some mending for us all
with Daddy in his straight cane-bottomed chair
Leaning precariously against the wall.
We worked and played — and studied — with a trace
Of child resentment but we always knew
Much tenderness and love were in that place
And we learned lessons nothing could undo.
There in devotion upon bended knee
We knew deep feelings of security.

Enjoying Nature

My Climbing Tree

Helen Blackshear
Montgomery, Alabama

In the artist the child is alive,
the poet wrote, and it is true for me.
My eyes trace the twisted limbs
of the old oak tree
and I seem to feel again
the rough-edged bark
that scraped my hands and knee.

Past eighty now, I walk with slower pace,
unable to climb into my perching place
yet memory's miracle finds me there,
feeling the sun on my face,
the wind in my hair.

The Year in Haiku

Marge Edde
New Market, Alabama

Wakening grains burst
microscopic blades of green—
emerald rebirth

Powdered sun-parched earth,
oppressively hot west winds
beget dry whirlpools

Mute corn-stalk sentries
guard the gold of autumn mums
against theft by frost

Brittle tree branches
glitter in frosty moonlight—
translucent jewels

Arachne and Me

Rebecca Henderson
Madison, Alabama

Clean windows and sunlight are made for each other. Periodically this possible combination drives me into a cleaning frenzy.

Over my kitchen sink, the window is double, and the space sandwiched between the window and storm-window is a challenge. This is where Arachne has chosen to homestead.

Perhaps she likes the southern exposure and of course a pleasant view. Maybe the warmth also brings an abundance of insects for her pantry. She dines at a formal table covered by a personally woven, white gossamer cloth, where queen-like she patiently sits in the middle. This goldfish-bowl dining does not seem to cramp her style. The leftovers, hulls from breakfast, lunch and dinner, are easily discarded on the white window frame below, where they gather like brown bones picked clean.

When my task is complete, I stand back in awe of the beautiful unobstructed view. Tomorrow morning the sun will greet me through a criss-cross of angel-like hairs. She never gives up; neither do I.

Today after firing my chemical-cleaner weapon, I saw her. There on the window frame, she lay in a puddle of the poison, her tiny legs waving in a death-dance. I was horrified.

Spider first-aid was not offered where I went to school and I did the only thing that came to mind. Into a glass of water she went and was stirred vigorously by my finger. (Well, I had to do something to dilute the poison.)

She floated limply to the surface. Oh no, I've drowned her! The water splashed into the sink where it quickly disappeared, but where is she? Dear God, not down the drain, I stared into the dark abyss. Oh, thank goodness, *there* you are.

Tenderly I scooped the poor drenched darlin' onto a paper towel and placed her in the nice warm oven to dry out, with the door cracked a bit.

After a few minutes passed I peered inside and was crestfallen. Arachne was not walking around in the fiery furnace. Indeed she had not moved from her spot on the towel. Sadly I removed the body but was stopped short by the sight of wiggly legs waving. I was overjoyed.

Convalescing in a familiar environment, to speed recovery, seemed indicated. Towel and patient were placed on the window-frame sun porch. Apparently bed rest did not suit her as she righted herself on all eight legs and left her bed for, I assumed, physical therapy.

Later, during afternoon rounds, she was nowhere to be seen. I thought, perhaps, she had checked herself out, but the sight of a small brown body crouched in a crevice answered my question. Somehow, I don't think she trusts me anymore.

Hopefully, when the summer sun beams again and a small, gray, cocoon-like ball appears in the protected upper corner of the window, followed in time by animated specks, I'll know recovery is complete.

The Needlewomen

Helen Norris
Montgomery, Alabama

She always said there were two worlds.
They came together at noon when she was
Walking back from church and crossed the creek.
Not God and angels, nothing at all like that,
But just another world that bloomed from this one.
Or was it the other way around?
Walking through the woods in summer,
Hair done up and catching in the leaves and
Sunlight, and the more she looked at this world –
Clearest of all at summer Sunday noon –
The more the other one was there.
Her path was lined with haw and burdock.
When she touched one on the right
Someone touched one on the left,
And when she crossed to touch one there
That other someone crossed as well.
Solemnly through bird and branch
They stitched the matching worlds secure,
Whipping together raveled edge
With curling threads of emerald vine
Abloom with beads of infant grape.

She stopped on the bridge above the creek
Where the needlewoman stood below
Locked from her in stillest water,
Hair caught up in leaf and cloud,
Eyes that dreamed into her own
Or was it the other way around?
And there the two worlds came together,
Not a seam to spoil it, dappled
Over sun and shade, like velvet
You could stroke each way to make
It dark or light. Yet like
The taffeta she wore to service,
Rippling through her prayer like laughter,
Shimmer shifting into shadow....
Heaven weave her worlds with joy.

The Tale of the Ill-Fated Poinsettia

Ora Dark
Auburn, Alabama

I didn't want to kill it. I had to, surely you can see that?

For a time, we were happy together. The perky, pink poinsettia with its huge blooms and lush, dense green leaves greeted Christmas visitors and relatives in the foyer. This was not a permanent position; it was part of the holiday atmosphere, period.

Deadline for dismantling the Christmas tree is Valentine's Day. Eventually all signs of Christmas must disappear, except for maybe a few needles under the rug and the Santa hat behind the couch. But the poinsettia was still alive. Was it immortal?

Though a few leaves and lower petals had fallen off, the poinsettia clung tenaciously to life. It had become an embarrassment. I thought plants committed suicide when they realized they had to depend on me for their very existence. In spite of the fact that I had not watered it since last year, it hung on.

Every time I saw it, the poinsettia gave me a gnawing feeling that something was wrong. For $4.97, you are supposed to have a plant with closure. Did *Good Housekeeping* magazine feature half-naked holiday plants struggling to make it to the summer issues? NO! If they can mutate poinsettias to have stripes, then why can't they have an expiration date?

By the end of February, I moved it to the garage hoping it would terminate itself in the dark sub-zero conditions. But it survived. My neighbors were putting theirs out on the curb, I could see the stems and deformed limbs trying to escape from trash cans and plastic bags. Others put them on their decks to die a ghastly, slow death before the next round of holiday flowers presented themselves for torture. Sadistically, I found myself kicking it to make the petals fall off but they only reached for me in eerie revenge. Would it live forever?

Though the savage, pointed petals glared and entreated me, I felt only revulsion and contempt. Plants should know their place. In desperation, I ripped it out of the pot and threw it onto the compost heap.

Now I have... dirt on my hands.

Wit

Marian Phillips
Huntsville, Alabama

A butterfly and a bumble bee
    Have the same artful quality;
But God must have been in a funk
    To design and implement the skunk.
Or perhaps He thought it more wise
    To show power cut down to size.

Caged

Georgette Perry
Huntsville, Alabama

Near blazing sideshow and Ferris wheel
in an old barn with grey eaves
they have gathered the wild from our hills.
Squirrels lie on their backs in the heat.
There are foxes, raccoons, an owl
with fierce golden eyes. His talons
tread the sawdust cage-floor. He spreads
and fans his wings, pale-feathered.
Rabbits crouch passive.
The bobcat is limp on his side.
His stub-tail twitches. His amber stare
follows passers-by,
follows me out into muttering night.

I see them all still. The fairground
is empty. Storm rumbles over.
Now the bobcat's eyes are all
black pupil. He stretches
and grips his claw-hands again and again.
Hunter and hunted,
killer and prey together,
from the truce of cages
there rises a great breathing dream
as if a forest sways up through the close air.
All night long the rain
blows wide in gusts and thunder
pours its avalanche down dark lost mountains.

Ordinary and Sacred As Blood

Lost Summer

Evelyn Hurley
Gaylesville, Alabama

The solitary egret, one broom-straw leg
knee deep in October's liquid brightness
stands, still as a sculpted icon,
his whiteness reflected among the tree branches.

Summer lives there, somewhere
just beneath the silver surface,
the summer that the butterflies grew smaller,
with stingy wings in muted colors – amber, bronze and brown,

the summer the hoot owl grew hoarse with questioning
and the dog, long mute, began to howl again,
the summer the goldfish shed his neon skin
and floated like a splotched leper
in the plastic lined lily pond.

That was the summer
the song of the turtle was only an echo,
the thread hung loose in Clotho's hand,

and the grapes were not so sweet.

Indian Summer

Jackie Cleveland
Pelham, Alabama

Warm weather
   has drawn us out
      to the river
where my people stood
   on sloping banks
      and gazed at the same
sun
   drifting lazily
      through leafless frames
   floating
bronze feathers upon the water.

I sift through clods of earth
   for arrowheads
while he piles brush
   in a mound
      on this tapered land
   where no man has dwelled
      before us
   except the Cherokee
      in clustered domes.

Pulled outside on an evening
    like this
they must have sat before
    a communal fire
        not just for cooking
            but for the comfort
                of the circle
under stars stretching ancient patterns
        across a cast-iron sky.

His eyes regard signs of night
    while I thoughtfully
        examine
            chips of stone
                by the waning light.
Quietly
    he has begun to gather
        sticks
            for a fire.

Bamboo

Helen Norris
Montgomery, Alabama

A bamboo hedge is green ribbons,
Bird lime and sparrow chatter,
Shavings of sun, freckles of amber,
Patches of yellow pale
And restless as canaries,
Echoes of twilight, liquid shadow,
Sighs of rain and breathless waiting
To be thick and thicker.

It is a clutter of conversations
In a tangle of all hours.
The calls of crows are caught in it
And sifting down to nestle
Among the infant shoots.
The chuckle of brown hens
Rises like vapor. At dew fall
It is sibilant and urgent with insects
Weaving a singing world for
Tender arrows newly born.
Its myriad poles are huddled
And haunted with memories
And intimate past knowing
And forthright to the common eye
But devious and ribbed with
Cold ambition to inherit earth.

Gentle With This World

Ruth Thomas Halbrooks
Birmingham, Alabama

Let me be kind and gentle with this world,
Embrace it, not with crushing arms, but eyes
That gaze on vast expanse of earth impearled
In space when ebon heavens tranquilize
The night with velvet peace and soothing psalm.
May I be sensitive to life and find
I can yet hold a petal in my palm,
A sunset in my color-conscious mind.
Let me caress the earth with open heart,
Enjoy each birdsong with attentive ears,
Watch tides that change by moon's magnetic art,
Feel gratitude as each new dawn appears.
Aware of all creation still unfurled,
Let me be gentle with this treasured world.

Red Clay

Susan Luther
Huntsville, Alabama

Finally, I taste it.
After nearly thirty years in the land of cotton.

After walking, driving, flying
twenty-eight years, nine months and one week

over land so beautiful to look at turned
for seed, cut for roads, scraped for malls it hurt.

The naked earth I put on my tongue after all tastes
ordinary and sacred as blood, as prairie grass.

Have I forgotten prairie grass? Corn, westering
above a dirt-dark, dustbegotten sea. Gossiping

to green like angels' wings
in the ocean of molecules that staggers the weaving wheat.

Nor will I cease remembering the unforgiving cliffs and majesties
of that Rocky place where snow falls commonly into the verses

of May, where sun falls, as if summoned by lucidity, upon the chorus
of standing stones some call the Garden of the Gods.

Why did you marry (I ask myself)
a man from your mother's humid country and move here?

Ordinary and Sacred As Blood

Oh, for a voice
like a prairie wind,

like blue water.
Instead, the gods

mock me with a lip-shriveling sauce of red-eye
gravy, country ham, an Appalachian
theme song and a mouth full of rust-colored grit.

Maw-Maw
and
Paw-Paw

The Day Grandmother and I Repainted Dad's Ford

Linda Strange
Huntsville, Alabama

It all started off innocently enough. My grandmother had come to stay with us for a week and was more or less in charge of keeping me out of trouble while Mom and Dad weren't around. I was 16 years old and had just learned to drive, so my grandmother had her work cut out for her!

One afternoon when Mom and Dad weren't home, I was returning from the library. As I roared up our driveway in Dad's big 1957 Ford station wagon, it began to pour rain.

Dad's windshield wipers were old and always smeared the front window. And since one of his side windows leaked, he'd told me to always put his car in the garage when it rained.

I could barely see the driveway in front of me, much less how to get that big car into our narrow garage.

I jumped out of the car and ran inside to get my grandmother. She'd know what to do. She came running outside with me and stood on the right side of the garage door, telling me how close I was to it as I eased the big car inside.

I stuck my head out the left window to help guide myself in, since the windshield was smeared. I kept hearing a grinding noise as I eased the car in, but I was hoping it was thunder.

After the car was finally inside, I got out to inspect it and found that I had scraped most of the paint off both doors on the right side! My grandmother said she'd hollered at me to stop, but I couldn't hear her for the pouring rain and all the thunder.

I was now in a PANIC and getting hysterical. Dad would kill me and Mom would never let me drive again!

Grandmother very calmly told me we were going to repaint the car and they'd never know.

"How grandmother? And with what?" Dad's car was a bright canary yellow. Where would we EVER find paint that color and that fast before my folks got home?

Grandmother headed straight for my brother's room and found some paints he used to paint his model airplanes. Sure enough, he had quite a few small bottles of what looked to us like canary yellow.

We hurried back outside, dried the right side of Dad's car and set about with tiny model airplane brushes and repainted both doors. The match wasn't half bad, but you sure saw it on a second glance!

I wondered how long it would take Dad to notice. I didn't have to wait long. The next morning, bright and early, we heard a loud bellow coming from the vicinity of the garage. It sounded like a wounded bull!

Dad came charging back in the house and demanded to know what had possessed me to paint the right side of his car that gosh awful yellow!

Grandmother and I both broke into tears. She sobbed that it was all her fault and I told him it was mine.

It was two months before they could get the car professionally repainted. The guy at the Ford place told my Dad it took a blow torch to get the airplane paint off those two doors!

And my brother, to this day, wonders whatever happened to all his daffodil yellow model airplane paint!

Annie and L.G.

Jan Martin Harris
Birmingham, Alabama

Parkinson's palsied and crumpled his left,
so he held the ladder tight with his right,
steadying it for her to climb
despite arthritic knees.

Our telephone rang,
Miz Mary calling:
"Bob, better come.
He's got the ladder,
she's on the roof.
Somebody's going to fall and get hurt."

From the subdivision,
the station wagon
zoomed over tracks
to the old part of town.
Serenely on the screened-in porch,
my grandparents rocked —
no sign of a ladder.
But way high,
up near the chimney,
I spied a brand new
shining shingle.

Why Granny?

Jane-Ann Heitmueller
Vinemont, Alabama

"Why do you wear aprons, Granny?" I asked her one day,
as I nestled on her lap, while resting from my play.

"Mercy child," she replied, "it's just a part of life. It's as
valuable to me as Grandpa's pocketknife.

When I wrap it on each day it makes me feel complete. I'm
Prepared to face the day, whatever I shall meet.

Sometimes it's a wiping rag to dry my dripping hands.
Sometimes it's a holding cloth to grasp the boiling pans.

Now and then it dries a tear or wipes a runny nose. It's a
Part of all I do, wherever Granny goes.

Carrying potatoes or the hen's eggs from their nest.
Snuggling baby kittens close and warm against my breast.

Wiping up the drips and drops that splatter on the floor. Oft
Times used to dust the table and there's so much more.

On a rainy day it's used to shield my head from rain or to
Take the horses lots of tasty, yellow grain.

Sometimes it's a help to open stubborn lids I grip. It can
Even hide a dirty spot or shield a rip.

It's been known to shine a shoe or dry a puppy's fur or to
Clear a mirror when the steam has caused a blur.

Best of all though, precious child sitting on my knee, it's
A place to nestle you and have you here with me!"

Grandpa Knew How to Eat a Watermelon

Kennette Harrison
Huntsville, Alabama

My grandfather was one of three Harrison brothers — young farmers on the wild side — who eloped with three Connally sisters. As they eloped, the Harrison boys and his Connally daughters were followed by my great-grandfather, carrying his shotgun, as in all good elopement stories, except this one is true.

My mother was nurse to a woman who confirmed that she was the daughter of the Justice of Peace who married the three couples — in his nightshirt — before the Connally father arrived on the scene. I think the closeness of our family has much to do with the subsequent double cousins, who looked like brothers and sisters. They all farmed in the same area and stayed close, dabbling in preaching, teaching and healing in their spare time.

I am three or four years old at a family reunion in the country, playing with my three boy cousins. My girlhood is tolerated solely because we are blood kin. It is very hot. We wear only our white undies. Grandpa has on his striped coveralls, but no shirt. No one has shoes on. The soil is soft sand, and the four of us are digging tunnels in it. Grandpa asks in his booming voice, "Who wants to go to the watermelon patch with me?" The boys jump up and down, shouting, "Me! Me!" I do not know what a watermelon patch is, but I jump up and down too. Grandpa disappears behind Uncle John's house. I sit back down to play in the sand until the boys shout again.

When I get up, I see a big animal that Grandpa says is his mule. Old Blue, the mule, is hitched to a plank platform with wooden sled runners. Grandpa says to us, "Get on, sit down, and don't stand up." The ride is very bumpy. I am scared and hang on to my oldest cousin, Howard Byrd. The sled stops. I am amazed at the mule's big ears and how they twitch the flies away. Grandpa takes us out into the patch, tells us not to step on the plants. He knocks on several watermelons with his knuckles. I have never seen a watermelon before. I don't know if there is something alive inside that will answer his knocking. "Want red or yellow?" Grandpa asks. I choose yellow, but I don't know what I will get that is yellow. The boys say red. Grandpa helps each of us pick out a watermelon. He cuts them off the vine with his sharp pocket knife. He gets one for himself too.

The sun is very hot. Grandpa helps us onto the sled and tells us to spread our legs out and make room for our watermelons. My watermelon is very hot, but I hug it hard, hoping it will keep me from falling off as Grandpa turns the mule and starts back to Uncle John's house. We stop beside the sandy driveway. Grandpa gets us situated in a circle with our watermelons. Then he asks if we know how to eat a watermelon. The boys nod yes, but I nod no.

Grandpa gets a big rock and puts it in the center of the circle. He cracks his watermelon over the rock, and it opens in the middle, like an egg. Red juice flies out on us, and we all laugh. Then he says, "This is the way to eat a watermelon." He reaches in with his big hand and takes out a huge hunk of the watermelon heart. He raises it to his mouth and takes big, messy bites. The juice runs down his arm and chin and through the white hairs on his chest. We hug our watermelons, laughing harder and harder after each bite he takes.

Grandpa cracks open our watermelons. We follow his example and see who can take the biggest, messiest bites. I do not know that I will ever again taste anything like that hot, yellow watermelon on that hot day with my giant grandfather towering over us, laughing and laughing as I look up to see seeds and red juice sticking to the chests of my cousins. I point and laugh too. All three boys point and laugh at me. I look at my brown chest. I have seeds and yellow watermelon juice streaking through the dust of sand. More and more of the family come until we are all together, laughing.

"Anybody else hungry for watermelon?" Grandpa booms. "Old Blue's a waitin'."

This is my first memory, a memory of my Harrison family, most of whom are now dead or scattered. I believe I have lived my life like this memory—cracking open large things that I do not understand, or that seem too big for me to handle, and then reaching in, not even knowing what the consequences might be, just trusting that I could handle them, and taking a bite right out of the heart of things.

My Grandmother's Story

Anne George
Birmingham, Alabama

Try living with someone sixty years, child,
there'll be more missing than a finger.
That's no lie.
And him saying, "Oh, Alice, I'm bleeding to death,"
staggering around like a stuck pig.
And me saying, "You are not,"
which of course he wasn't,
and going to fetch the coal oil.
But, you know, that man still blames me,
says I ruined his handwriting.
A plain lie.
Three-fourths of the blood was from that chicken
which nobody even noticed was still flopping around
and which the old fool should have held tighter.

I'll tell you this, though, about his finger.
When he quit pointing, things got better.

Dawn

Susan Luther
Huntsville, Alabama

Light comes early in this valley.
Birds rise, singing for the sun.
Red clay warms, cotton flings its green arms wide —
carpenter bees buzz newly-mortared holes.

The old grandmother wakes, searches
for her lost son in the vacant kitchen

crawls back in bed with a woman she doesn't know.

Grosspapa and the Crow

Jane-Ann Heitmueller
Vinemont, Alabama

A lack of companionship was one concern Great Grosspapa Edd Heitmueller certainly did not have as he performed his daily farm chores in the spring, summer and fall of 1948. For you see, Edd had been "adopted" by a large, black crow with mysterious red paint markings on his legs and feet.

Whether plowing the field, repairing broken farm machinery, planting and hoeing the garden, or feeding the horses, he was constantly accompanied by his feathered friend. Although the fowl arrived unexpectedly one spring day and disappeared that fall in the same manner, he left behind a host of tales which Edd enjoyed sharing for years with friends and neighbors.

One incident occurred on a clear fall morning as Edd worked diligently to repair a flat tire on his rubber tire hay wagon. Discovering, upon careful examination, that he must travel to Cullman from Vinemont for a tire patch, Edd placed the wheel bolts together beside the wheel. The curious crow sat nearby observing Edd's every move. Upon his return Edd was noisily greeted by the frantic squawking of his feathered friend as he paced back and forth along the eaves of the barn. The bolts were nowhere to be found!

After a thorough but fruitless search of the barn Edd began to sense that his jittery companion could solve the mystery. In a stern, commanding bellow, hands planted firmly on his expansive waistline, Edd glared at the sheepish crow and demanded, "Son-of-a-gun, you go get those bolts right this minute." With seemingly total understanding the crow spread his massive wings and disappeared into the nearby pine grove. Moments later he returned with a missing wheel bolt and placed it on the barn floor. With astonishment and patience Great Grosspapa watched as the crow made trip after trip as all but one of the bolts joined its mates in a pile beside the wagon wheel.

The crow not only observed Edd doing his farm work. That fall, as the family worked diligently gathering sweet potatoes, the crow joined the work crew. He would fly along the rows of dug potatoes, grasp a sweet potato string in his beak and drag or fly with it to the wooden crates. Once there he would deposit the potato into the crate along with the other potatoes.

The crow departed late that fall, never to return. However, he left behind a very special surprise in his absence. One dark, stormy afternoon the following spring, while struggling to repair a leaky barn roof, Edd was startled and overjoyed to discover a very unusual sight. There, nestled safely between the eaves of the horse barn, was the crow's nest. It was a literal treasure chest of colorful, shiny trinkets. Edd viewed a rainbow of glass chards, marbles, scraps of metal and to his astonishment, the one missing wheel bolt. These treasures sparkled as brightly as did Edd's eyes when he recalled, for years to come, the special antics of his friend, the crow.

Wild Foxes

Jan Martin Harris
Birmingham, Alabama

"Wolf Den" was what she called the farm,
but wolves were not what Grandma feared.
It was foxes — wild foxes —
red animals that ran at you
with lashing tails, gnashing teeth,
and yellow eyes shining bright
with golden foxy rage.
One autumn day, late October,
we walked to the spring —
a barrel catching water.
Dead leaves lay in piles
like dirty cornflakes that
crackled and crunched as we
kicked down the path.
Behind us came a scuffling sound.
"Listen!" she said, and we
stopped in our tracks.
"Don't you hear that — it's wild foxes!
Stand right still — don't go no further!"
As the scuffling noise came nearer, nearer,
she held my arm, we held our breaths,
poised on tip-toe, ready to run. From up the path
the sound drew nearer and then
we saw a head, a man's head, bent forward to walk,
a palsied hand beating rapid time,
Granddaddy, doing his Parkinson shuffle,
soft-shoeing down to visit the spring.
Was my Grandma disappointed?
No wild fox at all —
just our own familiar lamb.

Just Pray, Honey

Dianna B. Murphree
Pelham, Alabama

Pa-Paw always had a piece of an old truck. This one was red. My mother thought it was an embarrassment to the whole neighborhood, but to an eight-year-old it was a sheer delight. My sister, Kay, and I always begged to tag along with him every time he left the driveway. It was on one of those jaunts in the back of that old truck that I encountered my first childhood dilemma.

Pa-Paw called himself a contractor, but he routinely underbid his work and never seemed to make any money. On this particular day he was going to talk to a man about a new job. He had agreed in his easy-going, good-natured way to let us go. "Us" was Ma-Maw, Mozelle, Kay and I. Ma-Maw, my maternal grandmother, in the cab with him, kids in the back. Now Mozelle was not a child; she was our aunt who, due to a terrible illness as an infant, was brain damaged. But she had the mind of a child even if her body was grown.

So off we went, Mozelle riding in a porch chair, Kay's pigtails blowing in the wind and me, "Miss Outgoing of all Times" waving at every passerby. We were all careful to dodge the tobacco juice Pa-Paw spit out the window. I'm sure anyone who saw us would have sworn we were right out of the hills. No wonder mother was mortified!

Soon we arrived at a suitable place for a picnic. Pa-Paw would leave us here to eat, play and wade in a nearby stream. As quickly as we were unloaded and settled in, he left to conduct his business.

The wonders of God were all around us. The wind whispered secrets to the trees and the brook babbled on and on to anyone who would listen. Ma-Maw always packed everything but the kitchen sink, so without a doubt, we were in for a treat. We stuffed ourselves with the delicacies prepared by loving hands and soaked up all the grandeur. Everyone was having a perfectly marvelous time, when suddenly I let out a yelp and ran, tears streaming down my face, into Ma-Maw's arms. "What's the matter,

Honey?" she asked. It took me a minute to recover enough to get the words out. "Oh! Ma Maw!" I squalled. "I put my glasses on the running board of the truck before Pa-Paw left!"

Those glasses were brand new. I had been tested right at the end of school and found to be as blind as a bat. My parents had immediately taken me to Sears and Roebuck where I was transformed into "four eyes." I hated those ugly glasses! I was going to be a movie star. No self-respecting *femme fatale* would be caught dead wearing glasses! I already marched with the high school band, danced and sang in shows, and took drama lessons. Mother, to appease her strong-willed firstborn, had promised that I could take them off for all such auspicious occasions. But I had been lectured, reminded of the cost, and threatened within an inch of my life about losing them.

"Now, now, Honey!" comforted Ma-Maw, as only she could do, "Maybe it's not that bad. Maybe they're not lost at all. Just pray, Honey. Just pray!"

My grandmother was a saint. I know many people have said that, but mine really was! She knew her Maker on a personal basis and she knew the power of prayer. She taught us from the cradle that there was never a situation that couldn't be remedied by praying. I had heard her pray a million times but I didn't know if she ever got any answers.

Maybe I was too upset, but I don't remember praying. I'm sure I did though. I was too scared not to. My mother was going to kill me! There was no way for those glasses to be found with all the dirt roads that old truck had covered.

Kay, only five at the time, had been extremely quiet through this whole ordeal. Suddenly, she ran to me and said, "Don't worry! I prayed, and God told me your glasses would be all right. They'll be right there where you left them. He said they would!"

At that very minute we heard the truck. My shaking legs carried me down the road as fast as they could go. When Pa-Paw saw the terror on my face, he immediately stopped the truck. My heart was beating uncontrollably and my eyes were afraid to look. After what seemed like a hundred years, I finally reached the running board. I could not believe what I saw.

Ordinary and Sacred As Blood

There they were! Not one inch had they moved! But Kay was not surprised at all. "Told you," she said. "God never breaks His promises."

The rest of the day was wonderful. We laughed and sang all the way home. (And we didn't tell mother.) It was just the first of many times I would experience answered prayers as a child. There was the time I spilled black shoe polish on the yellow kitchen cabinets. Oh! But that's another story.

Cookies — Cookies, Everywhere!

Patricia A. Sibley
Mobile, Alabama

To become a Diabetic in one's old age,
In my Dad's mind, was quite an outrage!
He'd stop every day at the Home's coffee bar,
And load up his pockets at the cookie jar.

In his room he'd hide cookies all over the place,
Then give himself away by the look on his face.
We'd find them in his pockets, in the drawers of his chest,
Between newspaper pages, and tucked under his vest.

Whenever his blood sugar would go up quite high
We'd say, "Lay off the cookies!" and he'd give a deep sigh.
Then he'd clutch at his pockets and say, "Not even one?"
To him, this was like taking away most of his fun.

They got him his own jar filled with cookies and cakes,
But nobody told him they were 'sugar free' fakes.
He said, "They really like me, 'cause look what I got —
My very own filled-to-the-brim cookie pot."

He'd offer a cookie each time someone came in,
And if you turned him down, he thought that was a sin.
I can still picture him sitting there in his chair,
With both hands full of cookies — cookies everywhere!

The Lady's Garden

Patt M. Devitt
Northport, Alabama

The sweet smell of honeysuckle and wisteria draws me back to a garden I knew in my childhood like a lover beckoning for one more embrace. The Lady's Garden was at my grandfather's lake home on the banks of the Tennessee River in north Alabama, a place to read and daydream. My grandmother had planted this small flower and sitting garden near the main house and used it as a sanctuary when raising their brood of six active sons.

My petite, French grandmother planted her garden just across the gravel path from the screened porch of the house. She could be near her active, demanding household yet have a little privacy, too. A towering oak tree was an anchor at one side of the garden offering shade for the wooden swing, the *balance soir,* with two facing seats that swung to and fro at the will of the swingers. A brick path led through the garden and outlined rose beds. Honeysuckle vines wrapped around stone walls, wisteria vines climbed the oak tree.

I don't remember my grandmother, Aline, for she died when I was three, but relatives that do remember her say this genteel, romantic lady loved her garden. I can imagine her in the 1920's swinging in the *balance soir* with her good friend, Mrs. Thomas, a WWI war bride from France. I am told they chattered in French about their native country and raising children in rural Alabama. The ladies likely discussed and planned the terrace garden of roses, irises and sweet smelling shrubs my grandmother planted near the river. Melinde, the household cook, probably served them freshly squeezed lemonade or fresh apple pie baked on the wood stove only 25 feet from the garden.

Perhaps in this garden, sitting in this *balance soir,* my grandparents talked about family matters on sultry, summer evenings. They comforted each other when their only two daughters died in childhood and they talked about the joys and challenges of raising my energetic father and his five lively brothers while perfume from the rose bushes filled the air.

During my girlhood years the wisteria vines in the garden had been allowed to grow rampant up the towering oak tree, rose beds were crowded with weeds and the honeysuckle hedge stood unpruned. The light blue Confederate violets had jumped their borders and hid some of the brick path. Grandmother Aline had died and the garden had gone wild. Yet, the fragrance from the flowers she planted still filled the air with soft agreeable perfume. The untidiness of the garden only made this corner of the homestead cozier to me, a special place to be.

On hot, hazy summer days I would swing in the weathered, creaky *balance soir,* hoping to create a little breeze in the still air. Back and forth I would gently swing in the shade of the oak tree with lavender wisteria blossoms dripping from its branches. I could watch the brown wren build her nest under the eaves of the kitchen roof. The scent of Melinde's biscuits or fresh baked apple pie wafting from that kitchen window made my insatiable stomach churn with anticipation. Often I would bring some of those tasty, golden biscuits drenched in fresh churned butter and homemade muscadine jam to my cherished place and read. Or, I could just scrunch way down on the swing's bench and let the disorderly foliage hide me from pesky younger sisters.

Some mornings I snitched a cushion from the glider in the house and stretched out on the *balance soir.* I put my bare foot up on the rough side-bar to assure a steady swing and to get just the right pitch of squeaking vibrations. Here I read how Nancy Drew solved puzzling mysteries. During tense scenes I chewed on the ends of my straight, black hair or my ragged fingernails and the squeak of the swing rose to a higher pitch. Sometimes I imagined myself as Jo Marsh dealing with her boys, as I daydreamed in my garden haven. Here, too, I read about Elsie Dinsmore and discovered what revolting wimps some girls can be.

The *balance soir* was just the right spot for watching animal capers. Gray squirrels chased each other around the oak tree. Up and up they scampered, then daringly leaped from an overhanging limb onto the roof of the log cabin that served as the house's kitchen. Nesting red cardinals in nearby bushes or scrapping blue jays often caught my attention. If I kept the swing very still I'd hear the tapping, scratching of toenails hitting stone and see flashes of brown impish chipmunks playing tag through the stone wall under the honeysuckle hedge beside me.

Remembering this garden brings me the contentment and pleasure of old, proven love. *Merci beaucoup, Grandmère Aline, pour ce petit jardin.*

Prayer for my grandmother

Melissa Roth
Auburn, Alabama

Your hands
>   which have held me since infancy
>   I hold now in my own
>   Your fingers struggle against mine,
>   Patting out a distant rhythm

>   Your veins trace an endless landscape
>   beneath the greying paper of your skin
>   Hot eruptions of blue, coursing fast
>   against the weight of too many years

>   Do you remember
>   holding me now,
>   that summer, when you crouched behind me in the dirt
>   enfolding me in the wide span of your arms
>   holding my ten small fingers
>   in your ten great ones
>   guiding the simple movement of trowel against soil
>   as we turned back the fine grey earth to make a hollow
>   for the wrinkled brown seed?

>   or
>   are you lost
>   in this quicklime of flesh
>   living
>   only if I squeeze your hand so tightly—
>   in an effort to compress you
>   into the space of this moment—
>   that you collapse in on yourself
>   and the blood comes
>   coursing fast

Ordinary and Sacred As Blood

About Mac

Anne George
Birmingham, Alabama

To the best of her reckoning, Lettie Marbury had quit sleeping ten years ago when she was seventy-two. It hadn't bothered her much. She would catnap some in her chair and watch the PTL Club with the volume turned off so it wouldn't wake up anyone. It didn't bother her not hearing the program. What she liked was seeing how pretty everyone looked, even the men. She especially liked it when a whole bunch of people would collect around a fountain and she could see they were singing their hearts out and clapping their hands. She seldom catnapped at these times. Just when two preachers would be talking together.

Now it was six o'clock and a redheaded kinky-haired woman was mouthing, "Good morning. God loves you."

"I hope so." Lettie pushed herself up from the reclining chair and moved her toes around in her crocheted shoes. Her feet began to tingle and that was good. It was the days they stayed numb you had to worry about. She took a tentative step and then another. The hip she had broken when she had what they said was a stroke turned stickily in its plastic socket.

"Stroke, my foot," she said, remembering the day of the vision and the way the light went all fuzzy in the garden like she was looking through the kind of veil she used to wear on her hats. She saw the angel then, standing right there at the end of a row of pole beans, and it was when she started toward it she fell over one of the stakes and broke her hip.

"Lord, Grandma," Jim had said. "Looks like an angel wouldn't have let you hurt yourself so bad." And Lettie saw him smiling. But she knew what she had seen.

Don't slam the screen door. Wake up the baby. Lettie shuffled across the porch. A chipmunk ran between the geraniums and she wondered where Dickie was and then remembered how swollen the cat's belly had been the day before.

"Dickie has kittens in the barn," she said to the morning and knew it was so. She backed up to the rocker, placed both hands on the arms, squatted slightly, and dropped into the seat.

Fog still covered the river bottom. Little banners of it fluttered across the lower pasture. Wet morning grass in the front yard. Lettie rocked and smelled the freshness.

Mac wouldn't have it. He wanted the yard swept and that was the way of it. The toughest broom sage grew by the river. It clawed the dirt like chickens. Scratch. Scratch. No snakes to bite the children playing.

"The grass is growing," Mac said, looking out the window and she said yes and went on washing the sheets because she was too busy taking care of him to sweep the yard what with his mind coming and going and even finding him one day in Conrad's barn not knowing where he was. When he died she bought a lawn mower, one of the fancy gas ones from Sears. Lettie cutting the grass barefooted. Old woman with grass like mud between her toes and making her feet green. She smiled to remember it.

The screen door slammed. Donna with the baby. She put him in the playpen and smiled sleepily at Lettie.

"Morning, Gran."

"This is it."

"What, Gran?"

"July."

"It's September, Gran." Donna handed the baby his bottle, yawned and stretched. "I got the last of the butterbeans for us to shell."

"All right." Lettie leaned over and looked at the baby sucking the bottle. Sometimes she lost track. There was Mac the husband and Mac the son who had played in the dirt yard and was a fat old man and now Mac the baby.

"Mac," she said.

Donna smiled. "I'll get you some breakfast."

"How long you lived with me, Donna?"

Donna knew what Lettie wanted to hear. "Four years, Gran. Before that I was a school teacher, remember? And I bought all my clothes at a fancy department store in a great big mall that was like Christmas with lights everywhere. And every night I ate supper where you could choose anything you wanted to eat."

Ordinary and Sacred As Blood

"And why did you leave?"

"I met Jim and fell in love with him." Donna went in and shut the screen.

Lettie closed her eyes and thought of the shopping mall and the people singing on TV. Probably ate at that cafeteria.

Mac threw his bottle from his playpen and hit Lettie's foot. He had pulled himself up and was staring at her.

"Dickie has kittens," she told him. The baby smiled. "Healthy and in the barn, God willing."

God willing. God willing. God's will. Billy Graham said all the time God's will be done. And the little preacher in the black wig without a neck. And it was a puzzle. Was it God's will to have the doctor open up Mac's head and take out that growth? Two years of Lettie help me and Mac, I can't, and him dying by little pieces. And then his birthday with his mind clear and her making him a lemon cheese cake and putting the sleeping pills where he could reach them while she went out and picked up pecans. It was a good pecan year. It was. She had a croker sack full before she went back in the house. But was it God's will? She was about to ask the angel when she fell in the bean patch. Her hip twinged when she thought of it.

She shifted in her chair. It was going to be a hot day. The sun hadn't climbed as far as the pines by the road and it was already hard to breathe.

"It's going to be a scorcher," she said to the baby. Then she dropped into a half-sleep, half-dream. Her sister Emma was coming toward her in a white dress holding out a plate of ice cream.

"It's peach."

"I thank you, Emma." The sound of her own voice awakened her.

"Breakfast, Grandma." Lettie looked to make sure Jim was real. Then she held out her hands and he helped her up. The rocker creaked like a live thing as she left it. Like she had been sitting on a nest of crickets.

The old John Deere cap hung on a hook just inside the door. Lettie saw it as they walked in.

"Mac," she said.

"He'll be all right in his playpen, Grandma." Donna put a plate of scrambled eggs and grits before her. Muscadine jelly. Vines at the river.

Children swinging like Tarzan. Be careful. Be careful. And Mac laughing. Eating muscadines.

"I'm going to finish mowing the bottom field," Jim said. "Don't want it to start raining on me."

"I don't think it's going to." Donna turned on the radio. Jim grabbed her and they danced around the kitchen.

"Let me go, fool. Your eggs are burning." Donna slid from him slowly.

Lettie smiled at them. She had loved to dance. Whirling and clapping. Sometimes after a dance she had undressed sitting on the bed her feet hurt so much. They did. And around this very kitchen swinging the children, stumping her toe on the old iron stove and Mac and the children laughing. But it had hurt. Been blue for days.

"The stove is gone," she said suddenly.

"We have a new one, Gran," Jim said and Lettie could see that it was so. It had cooked the eggs she was eating. But it bothered her. When things were gone, the story went with them. Like the empty chicken nests in the barn. In her mind's eye she could see the chickens running to her call and the guineas. There was a stupid one named Henry drowned in a mudhole in the yard. She had thrown him in the river before the children saw. Stupid Henry. Floating down the river like a big spotted butterfly.

"Dickie has kittens," she said. "I want to take her some breakfast."

"Take her a big one." Donna opened a can of cat food and added breakfast scraps. "Think she's in the barn?"

"In one of the old nests."

"Well, you be careful. Hold the rail down the steps."

Be careful. Lettie slid her feet into canvas shoes and took the plastic bowl. Be careful.

"I hope we can give them away. We really ought to get her fixed," Donna was saying. Lettie opened the screen door and shut it quietly. The baby began to cry as she went down the steps.

"Don't cry. Don't cry. Papa's gonna buy you a diamond ring." She tried to sing the song on the way across the yard, but it hovered just at the edge of her memoty. Like having to look at the side of a star to see it. Don't cry.

The barn was dark and cool. The sun followed her through the door.

"Dickie," she called, and Dickie was there rubbing against her legs. Lettie put the bowl down.

"Where are the babies, Dickie?" But Dickie was eating. Nervous. Moving around the bowl.

"I'll find them," Lettie said. And she did. In the second empty chicken nest a small twining of black and white fur. She picked one up and it began to mew. Dickie came running.

"I'm sorry," Lettie put the kitten with the others. Dickie began to wash them. Licking them hard, rolling them over on their backs.

"I'll put your food up here." Lettie reached to get the bowl and saw a tiny body just under the chicken roost. Solid black. She picked it up. It was already stiff.

"I need to ask you about God's will," she told the angel who was standing at the barn door. She tried to hold the kitten out but her arm wouldn't work. She sat down abruptly, painfully.

"You see, I don't understand. Things are born and die and we do the best we can. But it's all a puzzle."

Above her head she could hear Dickie purring. The angel moved closer.

"That thing about Mac. I had to do it." And it was so. If she went to hell it was so. She sighed and her breath floated up through dust motes, through the open door.

Dickie looked up from washing her babies. But there was not another sound. Not one. She stretched and curled so each kitten would have a nipple. Then she closed her eyes and slept.

Celebrating
Our Spirit

Tap of the Spirit

Van Potter
Phenix City, Alabama

As the preacher pounds the high
podium with his fist and
gets into the high of his
sermon, Mother Parker must
rise from the padded pew and
prance on the carpet aisles and
flap her long, wrinkled, bony
arms and speak in a Tongue no
one understands the rapid
ethereal utterances, and
at eight I see obeisant
Seraphim in her gleamy
eyes and I wring my Sunday
school book and when she glides near
me, a Finger taps my sleeping
heart and fifteen years later
when Mother Parker dies, as
the preacher stands on a high
podium, a Finger taps my
waking heart and I start to prance

The Tearing of Lewis

Helen Blackshear
Montgomery, Alabama

"They's tearin' the sins out of Lewis tonight!"
His sister came running with frightened face.
"Why Mary," I said, "you gave me a fright.

"He told me those folks were a pitiful sight
and that old black preacher a real disgrace."
The tent shone pale in the white moonlight.

Like a mushroom sprung up overnight
it filled the meadow's empty space.
They were tearing the sins out of Lewis tonight.

They pulled out his sins in their holy rite
and pleaded with Jesus to give him grace.
The tent shone white in the pale moonlight.

His long black body lay stretched outright
as they called Jee-Jee-Jesus, swaying in place.
They were tearing the sins out of Lewis tonight.

Then Lewis hollered, "I see the light!
Blessed Jesus done give me grace!"
The tent shone pale in the white moonlight.
They were tearing the sins out of Lewis tonight.

The Baptizing

Kenney Greene
Auburn, Alabama

Last summer Harmony Baptist Church celebrated its centennial anniversary with an old fashion baptizing at Crooked Creek.

Until you have gone to an old fashioned baptizing in a creek and been dunked under (or I should say slipped under) you just have not experienced the real meaning of sin washing.

One June Sunday afternoon the congregation of the little country Harmony Church met on the banks of Crooked Creek to baptize sister Kate Langdale, sister Ruby Conner and old brother Fletcher Thomas.

The people started to sing "Shall we gather at the river, the beautiful, beautiful river," just as two dead fish and a bloated dead body of a skunk floated by. It had to be a skunk because of the smell and the telltale dirty white stripe on the slick water-logged, black body. Not to be deterred from their objective, the congregation went on with the song.

Preacher Kent preached a short sermon on baptizing and then after prayer he waded into the muddy creek until he was over waist high in midstream where he found a footing between two underwater rocks to wedge his feet to keep from being toppled by the swift undercurrent.

Sister Kate Langdale was the first to be led into the muddy rain-swelled creek. She found one of rocks to wedge her foot that Preacher Kent had his foot wedged between. In fact, her foot was on top of his. The water took most of her weight and being a little old lady did not put undue pressure on the preacher's foot.

"I baptize you in the name of the Father, Son, and Holy Ghost."

Kate's head disappeared under the murky water to come back up dripping water and something green and slimly.

Deacon Kerr proceeded to help sister Langdale to the bank where the good women of the church gave one loud gasp as she came out dripping mud and water. They scrambled in one large mass around Sister Langdale. The water made the white dress she wore transparent. Also, either because she never wore them or just forgot them, Sister Langdale was not wearing underpants. The ladies ushered her to a nearby car where they helped to dry her, slime and all.

Sister Ruby Conner's time was next. To be on the charitable side, let's say she was stout. Sister Conner had a dubious past and even though she was a changed creature she still sported her dyed, brassy red hair. Deacon Kerr proceeded to lead her to the middle of the stream where Preacher Kent was still wedged between the rocks. Sister Conner did not find the rocks to stand between but did find a slippery loose stone and just as Preacher Kent took her hand the rock turned, sending her and the preacher under at the same time. Then the current took over and both started down the creek, Preacher Kent doing his best to try to swim against the current and Sister Conner flinging her hands, with brassy red tendrils covering face and eyes.

"I can't swim," she screamed.

The whole congregation started running down the creek bank to save the two. It was a good thing an old footlog was across the creek and both managed to grab hold until rescue came.

No one ever mentioned how Sister Conner was taken out of the creek.

Old Brother Thomas was baptized two weeks later in the serene inside baptistry. Sister Conner did not return to Harmony Church. She became a Methodist.

Something He Said

B. Kim Meyer
Athens, Alabama

The Africa muse had captured him
Serengeti sage whispering
   through his veins
calling to a kindred note
music in a soul
searching for roots he
didn't know he missed...
I could hear the rhythm
   in his words
ancient drums
hear it in the music of his voice
Africa, calling him home
and he was half way there
   as he spoke

Vigil

Georgette Perry
Huntsville, Alabama

I hear them, I hear them all over the south
too old to bear but bearing in arms
grandchild or wastrel nephew's get, rocking
or barefoot on chilly floors, singing the night.
They sing a hillside, rocks under knees
of one who prays in mortal fear. They croon
in hoarse slow voices, *Night with ebon pinion.*
How dark it is! The angels have not come.
Tis midnight and on Olive's brow...
The sobbing baby catches her breath and listens.
Hush, child, hush. Gethsemane's blood-night
surrounds the house. The trees are loud with wind.
One time I heard a preacher say
(of the sisters, the thin one with deep eyes,
and the other, flour on her busy hands):
By the walls of the garden James slept, and John —
Mary and Martha would not have slept.
Mournful and sweet the song goes on, though directly
the babe in arms quietens, hiccups and dozes.
The women's voices are so low I barely hear them.
They've known the garden, waiting a traitor's kiss.
While Jesus prays the women will not sleep.

God Is So Good

Judy Ritter
Gadsden, Alabama

His little legs ran through the hayfield, feet parting the fresh blades of green grass that shimmered silver in the bright sunlight of midday. The breeze was cool on his tender face as it sometimes was on an early spring day in northeast Alabama. Christopher ran a few feet ahead of his grandmother, who shuffled through the grass, loaded down with a canvas tote filled with a beach towel and magazines in one hand, and a box of Christopher's matchbox cars and trucks in the other. They were headed to the "sand pile," a natural pit of sand created by the overflow of the banks of the small river which bordered the acreage owned by Gran and Pops.

Christopher was four years old, barely, and it was only recently that he had begun to show signs of fully appreciating the wonders of nature that a visit to the farm, complete with bugs and spiders and things, could provide. As he approached the widespread arms of the old oak tree and the familiar family picnic ground beneath it, he put his hands on hips and turned to face his grandmother, his eyes sparkling as blue as the sky above him. "I beated you, Gran," he said.

"Oh, no, you haven't. We're not there yet." She took off running towards the river, stepping over fallen tree branches, skirting sprouting May apples peeking their drooping heads through the sandy earth, and shouting, "I'm gonna beat you, Christopher." She could hear his squeals of delight as he whizzed past her, stuck in fourth gear, arms working as hard as legs.

"I'-m b-e-a-t-i-n-g y-o-u G-r-a-n," he said as he passed her and slid headfirst into the sand pile. "C'mon, Gran, take your shoes off and play with me." He had one shoe and one sock already off, and was pulling on the other shoe. "C'mon, Gran, take your shoes off."

"I'm gonna wait a while. I'm gonna sit here and watch, okay?" She spread her towel out across the sandy dirt next to Christopher, sat down, pulled out a magazine, and began to flip through the pages, starting from the back. She drooled over the colored pictures of flower gardens and mentally planned future plantings of her own garden. She lay back on the towel and felt the warm rays of the sun soothe away the layers of winter dormancy. Her first winter after retirement from public school teaching had been one of adjustment — learning to slow down, adapting to less activity, enjoying the still moments. She had made progress, but she still had a long way to go. She closed her eyes and listened to Christopher's car sounds, the busy twittering of birds, the wind talking through the trees, a crow fussing in the distance.

"Hey, Gran, don't go to sleep. C'mon and play with me. I know, Gran, let's walk in the water!" Christopher began pulling her up by the arm.

"Okay," she said reluctantly. "But you've got to get in the water, too." She slid off her shoes, digging her toes deep into the cool sand. "Oooh, that's cool, Christopher. Feels good, huh?"

"C'mon, Gran, to the water."

"Okay, c'mon down the bank over here. Give me your hand." She led him to the water which was clear and barely moving, tiny ripples interrupting patches of smooth reflecting glass.

"Do ya see any fish?"

"Are there some fish in there, Gran?"

"Yes, but they won't hurt us. I'll go first. Oh, it's r-e-a-l-l-y cold."

Christopher slid one foot into the water, wrinkling his freckled nose in disguised delight.

"It's squooshy, Gran." He put the other foot in and grinned. "It's cold. Cold and squooshy."

"Too cold for me. I'm getting out." They made their way back to the towel and sat down.

"Let's lie down on the towel, Gran."

"Good idea." They lay side by side, looking up at the tall tulip trees just beginning to show signs of life.

"This is so nice, just you and me, enjoying our own little beach."

"Yeah, Gran, this is so nice. Hey, Gran, why are there not any more dinosaurs?"

"Because there aren't any anymore. They died out a long, long time ago. The ones you see in the movies are not real."

"And are there alligators here in the water?"

"No, not in this water. Alligators live in BIG WATER, like at the beach."

"Can they get out of the water?"

"Yes, but they have to live close to the water."

"Oh."

They both became very still for a few minutes, looking up at the trees, enjoying the heat of the sun on their faces. Finally, she said, almost whispering, "God is so good."

"Why did you say that for, Gran?"

"What? God is so good? Because... God is good. He's letting me be here with my grandson... and He's giving us this great day."

"Okay, Gran, I'm going to say that now. You don't say anything, okay?"

He said, "God is so good."

She looked over at him and couldn't help laughing.

"No, Gran, don't laugh. Don't do anything. Let's do it again," he said in a very serious tone.

Silence, then a small solemn voice said, "God is so good."

She didn't even smile this time. She waited for him to say something. After a long pause, she looked over at him. He smiled, jumped on top of her, reached his arms around her neck, and gave her a huge hug. Then, just as abruptly, he returned to his sand pile without a word and resumed play.

She sat up, stuffed her gardening magazines back into her tote, leaned back on her arms, and watched her grandson. His mind was now a million miles away from her. There would be more moments like these, she thought. She had no need to dream of blossoming gardens; he was sufficient wonder for her right now.

To a Friend Forever...

Dorothy Diemer Hendry
Huntsville, Alabama

While mourning you, I saw a dogwood tree
Beset by lashing wind and freezing rain.
Poor little tree, I thought. It is like me,
Not strong enough to stand this mortal pain.

But when the storm had passed, the dogwood tree
Still stood, encased in ice, yet holding up
Each branch, each twig, each cryophilic cup
As though in homage to some Majesty.

And now on April mornings clean and blue,
The tree has opened every chalice wide
And lifts a thousand flowers white and new
Like glad hosannas for the Eastertide.

"Dear one," I say, "The tree is strong like you,
Transcending death as only Love can do."

Christmas Chrysalis

Rebecca Davis Henderson
Madison, Alabama

My pruning shears paused in mid-bite. There on the rose of Sharon was a big, beautiful cocoon. What a lovely gift, a meaningful symbol for this season of hope. Advent is not always so warm.

Soon the cold dark days, more typical of winter, followed Christmas. There were times when it seemed spring would never come, but finally March brought the brightness of daffodils, and April brought green leaves. The cocoon brought nothing.

For weeks I checked the bush every day, then discouraged, I'd ignore it. Could it be dead? Searching for a clue, I hoped the fibers at the end had separated a little, but no, nothing had changed.

Twilight was falling one day in the middle of May as I trudged up the driveway. My daily walk had drained me and for some reason I stopped there.

All the months of disappointment faded as I knelt at the bush. On a limb near the cocoon, with wings opened flat, as if waiting for something, was what I had been waiting for. Quickly I rushed into the house for a camera. With darkness descending, it was impossible to focus properly, but the flash recorded the moment.

My long vigil rewarded, elated and satisfied, I said, "Goodnight," to the beautiful visitor.

The next morning found my winged friend still there. Neighbors came over to admire and we expected any moment it would take wing.

Saturday is a busy chore day, but several times I checked the bush. This was puzzling. Why doesn't it fly away, I wondered.

Sunday morning found me up early to let the dog out. With sleep not long from my half-focused eyes, my bare feet wandered over to the bush.

As in a dream, too wonderful to be true, I gazed in disbelief.

Perfect mirror images were they, as I stood on holy ground. Creeping closer, I could see that "my" moth was the one with the fat round body, and her visitor had a long slender body. She had been waiting, receptive, and her prince had come.

He had been active, searching, and he had found her. The ancient energies of opposites were fully expressed in this sacred moment of wholeness.

Days later, I brought the simple gray symbol into the house.

> An empty cocoon now on the shelf
> A memory is all that is left ...

But that memory is still vivid almost a year later as Holy Week unfolds. The splendor of an exuberant creator majestically pulls out all the stops, frosting the orchards with pink and tossing blossoms like confetti, yellow and lavender, across the landscape. And when the dogwood burst forth like an anthem, my heart will sing the psalms.

The sight of the cocoon continues to remind me:

> An empty tomb beside the sea
> And hope was born for you and me...

Now this same joyful hope has put straw in my new birdhouse. Long ago, it is said, straw filled another's tiny bed.

The earth is ready.

The Potter

Helen Norris
Montgomery, Alabama

When the potter made this bowl for me he smiled.
Sometimes he hummed a song I'd never heard
But mostly smiled. He never took his eyes
Away, but once he did, to say, "You smile
For me." He had a foreign way of speaking
And was speckled as a guinea hen
With flecks of clay he wore as if they were
So many medals he had won in war,
And was moreover dappled with the shade
Of moving leaves above his head, until
He swarmed with all of it as if with bees.

And while he treadled furiously, he asked
Me, "You are smiling?" "Why?" I said. "Because
I make for you a bowl for holding happy
Hours." I was dizzy with the whirling
And the rolling of the clay, the way
It climbed his hand, the way it went the way
He wished. Or did he go the way it wished?

It was impossible to tell. The bowl
Was racing round him like a skater round
The rink. It flung the taste of clay into my mouth.
"I make it so you drink from it, not wine
But happy days. I make it big for that.'
And at the word he plunged his hand and swelled it
And I felt as if I carried here his child,
Till clay had climbed his hand into my throat.

He left off smiling then. He was gone down
Into the bowl, mud-spattered flesh and bone, and
Drunk with wine he found there, cheeks grown hollow
As he hollowed it and eyes like empty
Pools. I knew him thrown against the skin
Of it, his flecks of clay hurled into it.
The wheel that flew and caught us sucked us in
With sun and shadow, made us clay, made us
Adam, gave us Eden... Then it stopped.
He wiped his hands upon his apron, broke
A twig and pressed this dent into the round rim
Of my perfect bowl. "But why?" I cried.
And he replied, "I make it not so perfect
So the soul escape..."

Keeping Watch

Carolyn B. Buchanan
Auburn, Alabama

We watch our children with eyes that never rest, always at the ready in case of a stumble; secretly afraid no one but ourselves will help if they fall. This is especially true if the child is 'different'.

My youngest son was born with autism eleven years ago. This past December, I was clearing out the accumulated debris in his discarded back pack when I came upon a crumpled piece of paper stuffed into the bottom corner. It was an invitation to the annual Christmas program put on by the students and staff of Wright's Mill Road Elementaty, and it must've been in his bag for over a week. As I read the notice, I saw that B.G. had been given the coveted role of Joseph in the play. The expanding pride I felt as I read the news was instantly deflated by the sharp edge of reality. B.G.? Center stage? Representing the most nearly-perfect man ever created?

Disastrous scenarios invaded my thoughts, destroying the picturesque tableaux of the prepubescent Mary and Joseph in the manger, gazing serenely down at the newborn Savior. B.G. had an arsenal of inappropriate behavior, no doubt about it — odd gestures, bizarre noises, outbursts of frustration — threats to the angelic aura always inspired by scores of pink-cheeked cherubs.

I took a deep breath and banished the pessimism. After all, I had faith in my gangly Joseph, who'd come such a long way in his own hard journey, and faith in those teachers and students in whom I'd entrusted his care. I'd seen them close ranks before, protecting him and preventing disaster. I had to believe they wouldn't let him down.

I'd almost convinced myself that B.G. would make the most wonderfully reverent Joseph in the history of the school when he bounded into the kitchen to ransack the pantry like a Hun on a raiding party.

"I'm so proud of you!" I enthused. "This paper says you've been chosen to play Joseph next week in the Christmas program. That's such an honor."

He glanced up, his cheeks bulging with Waffle Crisp cereal. He looked like a squirrel storing nuts for the winter.

"Uhmm huhmm," he nodded casually. He apparently did not attach as much significance to the traditional role as I did.

I was a little disappointed at his lack of enthusiasm. When I was in grade school, I secretly yearned to be cast as Mary in the pageant. I certainly thought myself worthy to be cast in the lead. After all, my first name was even Mary. But every year the role went to Nancy Newmarker, a dimple-cheeked beauty with shining dark hair that set off the dazzling blue polyester costume. Her mother even let her wear make-up for the occasion. To this day, I resent Nancy Newmarker.

Well, maybe it didn't matter to B.G. that he was cast as Joseph, but it somehow seemed a fitting payback to me for all my frustrating years of being relegated to the angel choir. I tried again to initiate conversation about his upcoming stage debut.

"So.... who's going to be the baby Jesus?"

"Nobody."

"Oh. I guess you'll use a doll for Him, right?"

"No. Jesus isn't there," he said, as he bolted for the stairs and his Nintendo® game.

I grabbed him on the upswing. "What do you mean there's no Jesus? Where'd He go?"

"My wife's pregnant," he replied. He puffed out his chest like a rooster before he darted upstairs.

My first instinct was to laugh — he was every inch the boastful male. I puttered happily around the kitchen for a few minutes until it dawned on me that his comment could portend disaster. I knew our recent talk about the facts of life would come back to haunt me somehow... but please, I silently prayed, not at the Christmas pageant in front of hundreds of beaming parents with whirring videocams.

Four days later, the big morning arrived. I came early and nabbed a front row seat so I could get a good vantage point from which to observe B.G. (and from which he could observe *me,* should I need to resort to disciplinary signals).

One of the male teachers B.G. idolized tinkered with the sound system onstage.

"Can I help in any way, Mr. Keasal?" I asked.

"I think we've got everything under control... for the time being," he said, as we both heard an outburst of frenzied singing and clapping backstage.

Someone shushed him, and I sat down again as the auditorium started filling up with proud families. Then it hit me. I hadn't even thought to provide B.G. with an appropriate costume, other than dressing him in the bright red and green clothing the notice had requested. The camcorder was heavy in my damp hands. Too late now, I thought. I somehow never pictured Joseph as an elf in red and green, but there was always a first time for everything. I idly leafed through the Xeroxed program. There, listed under the cast of characters, was B. G. Buchanan... my special Joseph.

The lights dimmed, and feedback from the standing microphone squealed, focusing any wandering attention on center stage. My heart fluttered as Mrs. Tremaine, the school principal, started the proceedings with announcements and thanks to everyone for all their hard work.

The program began. We watched from the dark as our children, with their enthusiastic voices, breathed life into another Christmas. Songs familiar from my childhood soon gave way to the exotic chords of a Kwanza celebration. Resplendent in colorful shawls and brightly painted paper hats, the boys and girls exuded joy that ricocheted around the auditorium.

Thus far, I had not seen hide nor hair of Joseph. I hadn't heard anything from backstage either, to my immense relief. Everything was running smoothly.

When the tribute to Kwanza ended, the first and second grade choirs marched in, and sang traditional Hanukkah songs. When it was over, they filed off the stage — rows of adorable baby ducks. Finally, I caught sight of the Holy couple entering from stage right.

Yep, it was unmistakably Mary. She was discreetly pillow-pregnant. Behind her B.G./Joseph followed awkwardly, wrapped in somebody's brown chenille bathrobe, his hair cow-licked up on one side. The legs of

Ordinary and Sacred As Blood

his bright green sweatpants flashed from under the tattered robe. Mary took the bewildered Joseph by the hand, and led him to center stage. Another boy, dressed in an authentic-looking caftan and a sort of fez hat, entered from stage left, and the three stood silently, waiting for their cue.

The exuberant singing of the program so far underscored the plaintive first strains of their song, "Innkeeper." At the sound, B.G. started rhythmically swaying, as if he were the only one in the universe who could hear the music. I held my breath and crossed my fingers. Please don't let him look foolish...

On cue, B.G. turned to his betrothed, and sang the lyrics with the music:

Oh Mary, I know you're tired,
but there's no room at the Inn...

With those words, he gently touched Mary's stomach, and then patted her on the shoulder, before he tentatively walked across the stage and approached the innkeeper in the fez.

Innkeeper, innkeeper
please don't say no;
we've traveled far you see...

I watched as B.G. tilted his head up to the ceiling, as if praying for divine intervention. In that moment, my boy, who still believes in fairies and Santa Claus, became Joseph, earnestly pleading for the shelter of his family. It occurred to me just why B.G. was perfect for the part of Joseph. God saw in Joseph what I see in my son — an honest man with a kind soul.

At the end of the program, when he appeared for a curtain call, the audience stood and cheered. The entire school had given a very unique person his chance to shine, and the light of his sincerity was blinding.

I'd like to say the pageant ended without a hitch, but I have to be honest. As Joseph exited, he gave his rump a good scratching. Well, Joseph's allowed. After all... sleeping on hay can be mighty itchy!

Together, You and I

Patricia A. Sibley
Mobile, Alabama

Lord, help me to remember
That as this day goes by,
Whatever comes, we'll handle,
Together, You and I!

If I'm asked to make a sacrifice,
To do something really hard —
I'll say a silent prayer for help,
Because it's for You, my Lord!

I want to share my joys with You,
My hopes and all my fears,
Because You're always with me, Lord,
In happy times, or tears!

I want You always by my side,
Dear Lord, until I die,
And whatever comes, we'll handle,
Together, You and I!

Changing

the

World

Quagmire

Pat Dickerson
Lowndesboro, Alabama

Lash her with stripes, whip,
But softly, she bruises,
And it all runs out on paper,
    Yellow legal pads —
    Matchbook covers —
    Check stubs.

Name it, label it,
Then step out of it, girl.
    Blood is not ink
    But ink can be blood.

Ordinary and Sacred As Blood

Letter to an imprisoned Indonesian poet

Patricia Sammon
Huntsville, Alabama

This morning, out in the prison yard -- I know it was cold, and cough-
   ing bright,
but did you notice those crows along the barbed wire fence?
Raucous, indeed. But there was a kind of inky sweep to their wings,
   didn't you think?

That was me, writing out your name.
And their unsweet sound? That was me speaking your name aloud as I
   began my letter.
Keeps you real in this empty room.
An unmelodious pronunciation, I'm sure. Accented, and shrill.
You'd perhaps not have known I was speaking to you
if I could have appeared there myself, at that fence, — some stranger,
   gesticulating.

And, later, back in your cell,
where waiting no longer fills a period of time,
but is just the sour air that must be breathed in, breathed out,
the lungs losing count,
— do you remember those footsteps outside, in the hallway?
In a held sob, they did not stop for you,
but continued on, past your door,
growing fainter and fainter,
turning down one corridor, and then another, and never ending with a
   hinged sigh, a slam.
So you were left to wonder, as you breathed in, —'Who?' and breathed
   out, 'Why?'
I'm sorry to have frightened you.

They were just my several plodding sentences, begging your release.
I often wonder the same — Who reads my letters? And why are they
    saved, or thrown out.

And later still, as you sat with your back wedged in a corner,
you dropped your face into the corner of your two hands,
and found a small, safe darkness there, at midday.
That was me, on the other side of the world, folding my letter
into an origami wing.
You pressed your knuckle to your lips
just as I affixed postage:
a fine concordance. Some things need no translating.

I know that all day long, and into the evening
you hear the diesel muscling of buses going by,
and the useless car horns, and the grunt of trucks, speeding up.
The ordinary world, so obscenely close.
What banality, to have traffic jams
just outside the rock walls of an interrogation room.
It must have seemed to you that we received the news
of your disappearance without even looking up.
But the drone of that traffic — that is not indifference,
that is me, in my despair.
Feeling useless. Always sending you proxies — birds and shadows,
always miming in the dark,
knowing that you do not know.
That is my four-square prison:
Atonal and everywhere, and too vast to be escaped.

Ordinary and Sacred As Blood

I doubt I would have had the courage it took for you to become an
    enemy of the state,
writing that poem, taking that stand — knowing that one of those
    trucks
would eventually come for me.
But I'm sure of this. You and I are identical in one way:
either of us could have become that jailer who walks down your hall-
    way.
It would have taken just the slightest change in circumstance.
Just the smallest turn of a key.

So, with humility
I will try to work without hate,
trusting in this: that if a prison of rock were ever to encounter a prison
    of air
they would cancel one another out,
all the strangers commingling.

The Christening

Carol Case
Mobile, Alabama

On February 7, 1845, William Lloyd broke a glass vase,
ancient and priceless, on display in the British Museum.
A vase found at the site of a Roman tomb
and cradled alongside a corpse hidden
in the earth's dirty womb for centuries
until some archaeological midwife let it breathe.
And what is glass without light to shine through it?
And what does a vessel transport?
Ship cargo, pages in a book, water from a well?
Or some ancient Roman soul to Purgatory
where it waits to be unearthed, wiped clean of sins
and smacked accidentally by William Lloyd
whose descendants will never be allowed to forget,
will see in history books, encyclopedias, and
art journals how the most valuable piece
of glass ever discovered, ever created,
was broken by William Lloyd in a British Museum.
Beside this entry in the *Guinness Book of Records*
is a picture of the largest pane of glass ever created,
placed in the Palace of Industry in Paris,
by the way, and still intact
despite wars and teenage boys with rocks,
waiting for the day a delivery driver backs
too close or a crane operator turns too sharp
and reporters will satellite the news across deserts
of sand enough to build a million windows
because only in the breaking do we see the value of an object,
and we should thank William Lloyd for pointing this out.

Ordinary and Sacred As Blood

History Lesson

Natasha Trethewey
Auburn, Alabama

I am four in this photograph, standing
on a wide strip of Mississippi beach,
my hands on the flowered hips

of a bright bikini. My toes dig in,
curl around wet sand. The sun cuts
the rippling Gulf in flashes with each

tidal rush. Minnows dart at my feet
glinting like switchblades. I am alone
except for my grandmother, other side

of the camera, telling me how to pose.
It is 1970, two years after they opened
the rest of this beach to us,

forty years since the photograph
where she stood on a narrow plot
of sand marked *colored,* smiling,

her hands on the flowered hips
of a cotton meal-sack dress.

Experiment in Tuskegee

Van Potter
Phenix City, Alabama

"Syphilis Victims in the U.S. Study Went Untreated for 40 Years"
New York Times, July 26, 1972

Jeremiah Jones
May 28, 1970

Doctor Jim,
Time after time,
I lie on your cold, white table,
and let you give me shots
for the bad blood you say I have.
Yet the tiredness rides my back
and I can't work my land no more.
The chancre claws up
through the skin of my private place,
and the sores eat my face and hands,
make my wife turn away.

Dr. Jim Willis
May 28, 1970 journal entry

This morning, I reflect on myself,
that 10-year-old boy hovering over a faceless fly
stunned and lying in a white saucer
on a tree stump in the back yard.
I de-wing the specimen and observe how it writhes, jerks,
pops up from the plate like a kernel in a hot skillet.
I note it takes thirty minutes for the insect to die.
Then I open the door of my office,
look through glass doors and down the corridor
at the dusty sharecroppers
sitting on benches, papering the walls,
waiting for my wonder treatment.
I turn, nod to my nurse,
and she says, "Next."

The Burning of Jeffery

Michelle D. Guyton
Mobile, Alabama

So many times I passed him,
not saying hello,
avoiding his eyes,
evading his presence,

For he was not my equal,
dirty clothes,
stinking breath,
an extremely sour body odor.

Had he looked in my eyes,
he would have seen the words,
go home, old filthy bastard,
go away, old worthless man.

Not knowing
home was the old wooden shack
which sat on the bank of Sadie's river

It's furnishings
a floor made of splinters,
light from a burning candle,
and a cocaine dressed pipe
whose fillings exploded without warning,
scarring his face beyond image,
burning the eyes I avoided.

Watering the Sidewalk

Tina Harris
Montevallo, Alabama

They are watering the sidewalk
Hoping a skyscraper will sprout.
And why not?

We care for electronic pets,
Enjoy scrumptious meals from virtual restaurants,
Adopt illegitimate phones born from phone sex.

Bill Gates has joined the staff of the Mayo Clinic
To perfect the beeper-cell-phone-tracking-device-attachment-option
For newborn babies.

Now they are watering the sidewalk.
If they would use crushed brick fertilizer
A Chia Tower might pop up any day now.

For my sister together we make
hu-hu (Yellow mocking bird)

La Rora Shonnise
Auburn, Alabama

Dance storyteller
on high cliffs, beating black drums,
refusing white myths.

Father left mom - me.
Agili'si (grandmother)
avenge come blazing.

For civil rights I
too would die, hu-hu sageing
Black revolution.

Lord, being double
minority is chaos
for black cherokee.

Under the vernal moon

Margaret J. Vann
Huntsville, Alabama

Even good Christian girls get pregnant
(for all the nights under the vernal moon)
Look at Mary.
(Can you think of a more Christian girl? mother of God and all)

She was a good girl, but the Holy Spirit
filled her one spring and nine months later — there was Jesus.
(If Jesus wasn't a Christian, who is?)

It's no miracle that — what's a young girl to do when she gets
     the chance to save
some wild boy from pain.   Some wild boy that's preying
on those Christian girls in the warm spring nights
filled with the scent of flowers and spring and needs and sins.

Those boys they need to be saved from their sins.
(Haven't those girls been taught to go out and bring the word
     to the heathen?)
I mean look at the spring — with Jesus rising up and the blood
     and the sap
(Revival time down South — shouting and moaning)

Who else but Christian girls can ease those boys' way into heaven
(Christian girls have been taught what sin is — they know right off)
Who else but a Christian girl knows the fervor of God's love
Yes the longing to be one with God however He's manifested.

Yes the springs of life bring the babies of winter.
And those heathen boys into church to get married.

Just Ask Me

Susan Murphy
Birmingham, Alabama

It's taken me 40 long years, but I've finally stumbled upon what I really want to be when I grow up. Even as we speak, the business cards are being printed, my new letterhead engraved. As soon as the ink dries (and my check clears the bank), I will officially be: Susan Murphy - Consultant.

I have always felt that if people would just do exactly what I told them to do, the world would be a much better place. Here at last is an opportunity to make that my life's work. I have been handicapped in the past by the fact that I don't do confrontation well. I've always had the hardware, but not the chutzpah. What I needed was a job where people paid in advance for my advice, then followed it to the letter... no argument, no discussion. Voilá — Consultant!

I think the market is ripe for this particular business because nobody wants to take responsibility for making decisions these days. Take Congress for instance. There's so much finger pointing going on there, I'm surprised they can even order lunch. It's a consultant's gold mine. "What should we do about balancing the budget?" "How can we save Social Security?" "Is there really life after the Legislature?"

Given a few minutes and a little scratch paper, I could come up with alternative solutions for every problem on the books. And if my ideas don't pan out, hey, it was just an idea. At least Congress will have someone concrete to blame. You can't put a price tag on that.

Which brings me to my fee. A penny for your thoughts doesn't go very far these days. I'd have to consider the time it took to come up with each solution, the hard core research involved, and any expenses incurred along the way. Basically, if I have to look up a word, I'll want time and a half. And I usually think better on a full stomach... at the mall... wearing a brand new outfit. If Congress doesn't have a problem paying $400 for a hammer, I can't see why they would quibble over a lousy pair of Armani heels. Stick them in the defense budget under the heading of "Things We Hope We Won't Be Called Upon To Defend".

Voice without responsibility. Audience without atonement. The First Amendment with no strings attached. It's the new American dream. Of course, if Demon Consequence ever does rear its ugly head, I can always declare Chapter 11, write a juicy tell-all book or claim temporary insanity. In any case, I'll be the darling of the talk show circuit.

I'm excited about this new consultant phase of my life. Only in America can a middle-aged woman from suburbia go on to become the confidant of the confused, the champion of the ill-advised, the scapegoat of the unprepared.

But what can I tell you? Good business is all a matter of giving people what they want. And right now most people want nothing more than to say, "It's not my fault!" If this trend continues, I may have to franchise.

To One I Know

Frances Cooper Smith
Montgomery, Alabama

A monument to what you think
You lift your shining strength so high,
I stand discountenanced to face
Your tall assurance in the sky.

Discountenanced I covet you
The sturdy slabs of granite thought
By which the pattern of your mind
In stately ordered plan is wrought.

I covet you the pattern plain
That labels proper and amiss,
And all experience you meet
Explicable in terms of this.

I look to you and turn away
That you should be so sure and strong
Who cannot make my crooked blocks
Build anything for very long.

A monument to what you think
You rise to such a splendid height,
I count it most irrelevant
To ask if you be wrong or right.

Ma Nature Takes a Twist

Helen Blackshear
Montgomery, AL

Alabama Heritage magazine, Summer1995, L. I. Davenport:
Although posing as simple herbs, jack-in-the-pulpits actually
follow a complex sexual scenario... Large, healthy ones,
capable of sustaining offspring, will be female; smaller and
less healthy ones will be male, and marginal ones will 'choose'
not to reproduce at all.

The Jack-in-the-pulpit flower
can change its sex at will.
When it's tired of being Jack
it becomes a Jill.

If the soil is thin and poor
a male is of no use —
so Jack becomes a female
so it can reproduce.

It makes me wonder if Ma Nature
by this crazy twist
is giving us a little hint
that she's a feminist!

A Mother's Ghazal

Mary Carol Moran
LaFayette, AL

I cannot see the war dead in their silent tomb,
But I have watched the beat of new life in my womb.

I cannot smell the hunger of a continent,
But I have ached from the emptiness of my womb.

I cannot taste the richness of celebrity,
But I have shone with pride for the toil of my womb.

I cannot count up the tears of homeless children,
But I have cried in fear for the child of my womb.

I cannot fathom the greed of corporations,
But I have cramped with the neediness of my womb.

I cannot pray to Mary with my good neighbors,
But I have rested with the goddess of my womb.

Dismal

Michele Debnam
Phenix City, Alabama

We make horror natural
And evil habitual

We cannot face
Bloody disgrace

So we lie with precision
Anger a daily decision

Dark loser
Drunken bruiser

We become what we hate
In darkness lost because we hesitate

letter to the system

La Rora Shonnise
Auburn, Alabama

I curse the man that took
away,
my past identity
when he pinned me down and tortured me.

And no,
I'm not speaking metaphorically. They let him run free
because of the whiteness that he has over me.

The district attorney said "I'm sorry, there's no way in hell
we'd win."

To the system:
don't blame me
for the warrior I've become.

It was you who made me numb.

Rising to the Occasion

Linda Frost
Birmingham, Alabama

She's been saving up for a sex change,
getting ready for her new name.
She's been cutting front slots
in her panties for years; time
to put something there. She's
got some work to do, a head job,
a final nod to ladies rooms and
the sit-down whiz. It's a new phase
in her chromosomal life and she'll
awake refreshed, fleshed
out of a tyranny of tears.
She's always had something
to add but she knows less means
just what it says. More is what
she'll collect from the letters
on her license and the buttons
on her fly. She may even ask
the boss for a raise. *Hey* —
she'll say — *see what I got?*
Less is just what it says,
she tells her mom, and calculates
the cost of a foreskin: if hers
comes circumcised, will she get it
cut-rate? *Boy oh boy,* she thinks,
I hate to pay twice for what's
always been mine. Boy oh boy,
she says, *boy oh boy oh boy.*

Saying Goodbye

Home Alone on Halloween

Deryl F. Barnhill
Northport, Alabama

His gnarled fingers trembled as he counted out three one dollar bills. He no longer had a billfold. It was too difficult to reach his back pocket, so he kept his crumpled bills and coins together in the change purse always carried in his front pocket. He smoothed two bills and as he unrolled the third bill, his trembling hand knocked his walking cane away from the counter where it was propped. His ears heard the fall but his eyes couldn't follow the cane as it slid beneath the toe lip of the counter. His crooked back could not bend down to retrieve the cane, nor could he straighten up enough to walk without the walking stick. He was trapped.

The young clerk of the Jiffy Mart appeared distraught. The cash drawer was open to receive the $2.14 the old man owed. Her instructions were never to leave the open drawer. She shot a panicky look around the store. Mostly the customers were folks who lived in the neighborhood, but few even knew the old man's name. Since his wife had died many years ago, the old man lived alone. In desperation the clerk called out, "Can someone please help?"

A young woman stepped forward to lift the cane and restore it to its standing position beside the counter. "Thanks," the old man murmured in a gravelly voice as he took his change from the counter, picked up his two bags of chicken feed candy and shuffled slowly toward the door.

Someone whispered, "That old man is pitiful. He lives alone."

Suddenly a small hand tugged at the old man's elbow, "Mister, are you buying candy for Halloween?"

Watery eyes, glazed and hardened by years, looked down into the serious face of a young child.

"Yes." His face softened as he gazed into the innocent eyes. His wavering steps pointed toward the door, where an incoming customer stepped aside.

With a worried look the child darted out the door after the old man, "Mister, mister, are you scared to stay home alone?"

Before the old man could answer the mother grabbed the child, scolding, "Stop that talk this minute. You've said enough!"

Retracing his faltering steps down the short path home, the old man wearily mounted the short stairs. Each step intensified the pain in swollen joints. He said aloud, "I'll just sit here tonight on the porch and wait. I'll be ready before the bell rings." After skipping a beat, the heart picked up again, and laborious breathing continued. "I'm so tired," he said to no one in particular because there was no one to hear.

Evening shadows softened as street lights appeared. Small costumed figures filled the neighborhood, followed at a discrete distance by watchful parents. Porch lights welcomed as tiny voices chirped, "Trick or treat!"

Back and forth up the path to the old man's small house the childish feet pranced — excited by each new candy corn falling into the plastic pumpkins. Prompted by adults from the street some children returned to shout, "Thank you!"

Then came the serious child. Cautiously edging up the steps and close to the old man, he said "I saw you at Jiffy Mart today."

The old man smiled and murmured an unintelligible reply.

The child continued, "You are not scared to be home alone on Halloween. Someone has come to keep you company." As the serious child spoke, a shimmering glow began to appear behind the old man's head. His white hair became silver and beautiful.

A frantic call from the mother on the sidewalk caused the serious child to turn and move reluctantly down the steps. As she pulled the protesting child along, his words tumbled, "Mommy, mommy, I saw an angel. I saw an angel, a big beautiful angel on the porch with the old man! Oh mommy, please come back with me and see the angel."

Unnerved by the serious child, she responded, "Be quiet. That's no angel. Your head is too full of spooks, goblins and ghosts. You have seen too much of Halloween. Come, we're going home!"

"But mommy, you don't understand. The old man is not alone on Halloween. He's really not alone. Please come back and see the beautiful angel!"

Those were the last earthly words the old man heard.

Last Visit with Your Grandmother

Barbara Kaiser
Crane Hill, Alabama

Rising slowly, ever so slowly,
Baba came to meet us at the door.
"Next time when you come, I hope
I am not so tired," she said.

"Oh, Baba," you murmured and held
her tightly.

"Dear," she began, "I wanted you to see
me with my hair fluffed, with
mahogany lips and nails to match."

You smiled and let her go.

"I like those gold slippers
so much," she said.
"You know, the ones
you gave me last year for Christmas —
Oh, my, that was a grand Christmas
wasn't it? You do
remember, don't you, Baby?"

You led her to a chair; I sat beside her.
You reached for her hand.

"That was the same Christmas," she said,
"that Mary Grayce gave me the lavender gown
with rosettes on it. Why, only last night
I had that gown on and Daddy
made me lie down on the divan.
He rubbed my feet with oil and rosewater."

You hugged her close
and held her in your arms.
"Oh, Baba," you said,
"I love you so."

We sat together for
a long time
without speaking.
At last she broke the silence.

"Oh, honey," she said,
"I hope next time when you come
I am not so tired."

Photographic Memory

Kimberly D. Martz
Auburn, Alabama

My maternal grandmother wore red lipstick to her funeral, a color
she never pasted to her lips in life, just as she never pretended
to like the simpering frocks they had her laced in then, its flowers

a mockery — just as those that stood in suspended animation in
vases and pots — of her vegetable gardens, miles upon miles of
wheat fields she and grandfather sowed and harvested each year

until the desire for rest and simpler patterns of growth took hold:
there the blueberries, and over there a row for peas. Smaller plots
of earth for backs that had not yet tired of seeing the produce of

hard work. Yet there she was, wrinkled face indignant under the
weight of strange make-up. Her hair curled in tight, grey ringlets,
she looked like a very old child, fingers balled and ready for hitting:

the nursing home bed was hard. I know. I watched her lying on it
every summer, her plain lips moving but uttering no words I could
understand, eyes pushing out pain. Nurses came and joked with

her, told her stories meant to make her forget she was dying, but
there wasn't anything they could do but turn her, rotate her
withering body like bald tires on a Ford 150. When we finally

shoveled the dirt over her, I sat silent in my chair, twelve years old
and licking a cherry lolly-pop. I knew she was dead. I knew what
it meant. What I wanted to find out was who she'd been before

the wheat fields disappeared, before the wheelchair became
necessary. Before her back began to ache with the knowledge that
death would sit with her for seven years in a small home that did

not belong to her. Now if I take out the old photos and turn them
in my hands, feel the worn paper, I can almost remember the touch
of her fingers, thin and shaking with the effort of reaching beyond

pristine white sheets. I can press them to my face and hold her
breath in mine, see the frown that might have been a careful smile
caught between her teeth. Closing the trunk, I can almost hear

her rusty voice, creaking in protest as I close the lid.

Hush, Child

Deryl F. Barnhill
Northport, Alabama

"Mama, why are we standing around grandpa's bed?"

"Hush, child, grandpa is dying."

"Why are my aunts and uncles and cousins here? Why do we need so many people here for grandpa to die?"

"Hush, child. Grandpa and grandma are getting married."

"Is that why the priest is here?"

"Hush -- they want to be married when grandpa dies."

"Why?"

"Because grandpa wants to have church mass. He wants to be buried in the church cemetery."

"Why?"

"So his soul won't go to hell."

"Look, mama! His hair spreads out like an eagle's wings on his pillow. It is white as an angel's."

"Hush, child."

"Mama, I can't see. The sun is dancing on the crucifix over grandpa's bed."

"Move closer to me, child."

"Mama, I see the picture of the Blessed Mother next to the crucifix, but I can't read the numbers. Please read them to me."

"It says November 16, 1934."

"Is that today?"

"Yes, child."

"There are more big words, Mama."

"Brownsville, Texas."

"Mama, the crucifix blinds me."

"Move in front of me."

"Mama, hold my hand. Now I see grandma's rosary — she is turning the beads. Oh, mama, look at grandma! Her dress is beautiful — it looks like pink cotton candy. Her ear drops look like little pearls falling on top of each other."

"Hush, my child."

"Mama, look at grandma's hair. It sweeps up like the river running backwards. Her beautiful comb looks like the sun shining through river foam."

"Hush, child. The priest is speaking."

"Is he marrying grandpa and grandma? I can't hear him."

"Hush, child."

"Mama, look how skinny grandpa's hand is. He is reaching out across the bed to hold grandma's hand. Look at his bones. His arm is blue."

"They are getting married. Listen."

"Grandma is holding grandpa's hand. He is smiling but his fingers have slipped away."

"Hush, hush — now they are married."

"Mama, why are you crying?"

"The priest is motioning us out."

"Mama, I want to get closer and touch grandpa."

"Come child. The priest must hear grandpa's confession. It is very private."

"Why?"

"Because this is the only time the priest can ever hear grandpa's confession."

"Why?"

"Grandpa is dying."

****

"Mama, where are we going?"

"Come child, outside the house. There are so many people here."

"Mama, I thought grandpa and grandma were already married."

"No, child, the church didn't see fit to marry them before today."

"But, mama, grandma told me she had 15 babies."

"Yes, child."

"And she told me she and grandpa cried as they buried little babies, and little children. Six times they followed a little casket through the dirt path to the church cemetery."

"Mama, why are you crying?"

"Grandpa is dying."

"But everyone is whispering, Mama. Why did they never get married before? They love each other very much."

"Yes, I know. But the priest would not marry them."

"Why, mama?"

"Because when grandma was thirteen her mother arranged a church marriage for her with a very rich man. Her mother did not know he was mean and cruel. He beat grandma."

"Did she run away?"

"No, her mother heard about it. She drove a horse and buggy many miles and found that your grandma was three months pregnant. Her mother raised her buggy whip at the husband, shouted at him and brought grandma back home."

"Where was grandpa?"

"He was married to grandma's sister, Pilar. Pilar died when her baby boy, Jesus, was born. Grandma's mother took care of the little boy, and soon grandma's baby girl, Lupe, was born. Then Grandma's mother had two baby grandchildren to look after. Grandpa came often to see his little son."

"I think grandma and grandpa loved each other way back then."

"Child, you are very perceptive."

"What does that mean?"

"Yes, they loved each other. But the church said they could not marry."

"Why?"

"Because grandma had a husband who was still alive."

"And did grandma and grandpa make a family anyway?"

"Yes."

"I don't understand. Why can they get married today?"

"Because I went to Mexico and searched church death files, until I found the name of grandma's first husband. Last week I found his name in the Iglesia de Virgen Maria at Valle Hermosa."

"Is that why you went to Mexico so many times last year?"

"Yes, yes, now be quiet."

****

"Mama, are we going back into grandpa's room?"

"Yes, the priest has heard the confession."

"Why is he still here?"

"The priest want to have the Holy Eucharist."

"What is that?"

"Communion."

"Oh, why does he want to do that?"

"Grandpa is dying."

"Mama, I want to stand close to grandpa."

"You can move up nearer to his bed now. Leave room for grandma to be the closest of all."

"Mama, grandma is moving back to the chair by his bed."

"Listen now to the exteme unction."

"What's that?"

"That is for grandpa because he is dying. Now his soul is safe."

"Can grandpa's body be carried into the church for mass? Can he be buried in the church cemetery near his six babies?"

"Yes, my child,"

"Mama, why are you crying? I think I am crying too."

"Hush, child."

"Mama, why is the priest telling us to leave again? I don't want to leave grandpa."

"The priest said grandma wants to be alone with grandpa."

"Why?"

"Grandpa is dying."

"She is rubbing his arm and speaking softly. I can't hear."

"You have no need to hear. Come child."

"Mama, don't rush me. Grandma is crying. I feel sad. Grandpa's hand is wet with her tears."

"Come, child."

"Yes, mama, I am coming... Mama, look, the sun is going down and there is beautiful gold over the river."

"The Rio Grande is always beautiful, but never like today."

"Mama, how can grandpa marry, confess his sins, take communion, receive final rites, and die all in the very same day?"

"Hush, child."

Hyphen

Maggie Geist
Tuscaloosa, Alabama

Separating birth from death
a short line

1939-1999

sixty years
of laughter
and tears
so short

the going from here to there
from there to here
the doing

the caring
Oh, that hyphen
seems no longer

than a dash

Dialogue with Death

Helen Blackshear
Montgomery, Alabama

Come softly, Death and take me unaware.
Let me not burden those that I hold dear
With long-drawn hours of agony and fear.
Spare me from more pain than I can bear.
Let me slip quietly away, nor let me share
My time of going. When that day draws near
Grant that I go with grace. Let it appear
I merely sleep. This is my deepest prayer.

But oh, dear Death, I beg you to delay
Your coming, for I have so much to do,
So many books to read and friends to see,
So much to crowd into each precious day,
So many songs to write and scenes to view
Before the silence of eternity.

Yes

Alison Wright Franks
Auburn, Alabama

At 4:20 a.m., Patt's father called from the hospital to say that our son Patt's pupils were fixed and his brain waves had ceased. It was over.

People said to me, "It's the most awful thing." But it wasn't the most awful thing. To not have had Patt in our lives would have been the most awful thing. My memories are what get me through the hardest days.

I remember Patt when he was three and picked the first bloom of a neighbor's prized geranium and brought it to me. I put it in a wine glass, pulled out my pastels and sketched it. I titled it, "Love Gift."

I remember him at five when he ran out of our motel room in Selma, Alabama, across the grass to the pool, off the diving board into the water. A little old man, dressed in a suit and tie, walking with his wife to dinner, jumped in to "save him." He was a little thing, but he had been swimming since he was three.

I remember him at six when he came running into the house and asked me where he came from. I sat him down and started telling him about Daddies loving Mamas so much that they wanted to be part of them and... He cocked his head to one side and said, "No, Mama. Where did I come from? Dale came from Hubbertville."

I remember him at seven when he begged me to let him take six dollars out of his savings account at the bank and wouldn't tell me what he needed the money for. He was so insistent that I finally agreed. I drove him downtown where he bought a chintz back rest, pale yellow with pink cabbage roses — for me. He said, "You liked that Mama, and you don't ever buy anything for you, so I did."

I remember him at ten, laughing his head off when I inquired as to whether or not anyone else had had an upset stomach during the night — after I inadvertently ate the X-Lax laced, chocolate iced, vanilla wafers that he had prepared especially for his stepsister.

I remember when, at fifteen, he and his friend, Larry, invited me to lunch at the Pizza Hut and he chose Lionel Ritchie's "Still" to play on the jukebox. I had been a widow for one week and when the song started I couldn't hold back my tears. Patt felt terrible over his selection. The problem was simply one of timing — I wasn't able, yet, to keep my composure. Today that song still makes me cry, but now it reminds me of Patt and our lunch at the Pizza Hut.

Sometimes when the grief seems almost too much to bear, I only have to stop and remember. When I miss him, I look into my heart and he is there. I have much to be thankful for.

I am thankful that Patt, according to the doctors, did not suffer.

I am thankful that he was happy.

I am thankful that our relationship was good and no things were said or not said that I regret.

I am thankful that he knew how much I loved him.

If, when Patt was born and placed in my arms, I had been told, "He's yours, but only for 23 years. Do you still want him?" the answer would have been, "Yes."

Moving On

At Least Once

Marian Phillips
Huntsville, Alabama

Prudence provides our pillow.
  Diligence kneads our bread.
Yet we should meet Indiscreet
  At least once before we're dead.

Lists

Alma V. Sanders
Huntsville, Alabama

List of Lists

I made a list of my lists last night
and a list of my lists of lists

Then I stayed awake all night
wondering what I'd missed

Tomorrow's Do-List

if your today's
    list of things
        to do tommorow

is the same list
    as your yesterday's
    'tomorrow's-do-list'

then you know
    you didn't do
        anything today

Graduating

Virginia Gilbert
Madison, Alabama

If I lived my life twice,
would I this time keep
my mouth shut?
Would I take my training
in biology and end up
selling real estate?
Or would I become
the campus radical
who is now an accountant?
Would I be the person
to address the graduating
class or would I sit
on my porch at 3 a. m.
letting my kids run wild?

People in my class
have been dying,
just two this year
in the "Alumni News."
Earlier, they were
"Weddings," "Tiny
Tigers," or some
other mascot.
Did they get what
they wanted, the liberal
and the realized?
Were they big donors,
upstanding members
of whatever, or broken
with marriages, wanderers
across the land?

Ordinary and Sacred As Blood

My past calls me
to reunion, to the President's
breakfast, and the
graduation luncheon.
And what did I graduate
to? Like the old faculty,
I am 25 and counting.
One said, "It's the little
stupid things that change
your life." And so
I am waiting for the change,
the stupid thing that knocks
me on the head and places
me on the Honor Roll
calling me to new life,
calling me to new life
before there is none left.

Dementia

Sallie Drake Scott
Huntsville, Alabama

It started.
She sat. She sighed.
She remembered her mother
sitting quietly
hands folded
blank stare
void of conversation
occasionally sorting buttons
in her starched white apron
surrounded by family
yet alone
in her world,
finished
with this life.

Day After Solstice

Elizabeth Frye
Birmingham, Alabama

Cold
I sit on the porch
wondering
why the noise has disappeared

Alone
I sit with the sight of my breath in mid-air
as my only companion.

I seem to have
forgotten
the meaning of summer and of
all things warm and golden.
I know that winter started here yesterday.
I cannot recall when it began
in me.

Winter at the Inn

Joanne Ramey Cage
Birmingham, Alabama

My merry Muse departs, with all her train
Of sweet beguilers. Fare you well, O Joys
And gentle Smiles; brave banisher of pain,
Stout Laughter; all you valiant natural foes
Of this old man Despair. Come back in Spring.
And I will entertain you with the crumbs
This grimmer guest, who cannot smile or sing,
May overlook; and when the Summer comes,
We'll turn him out, we'll laugh him off the place—
Together we can do it, you and I—
Alone I am no match for him; his face
Defies me to evict him. With a sigh,
Spreading his bed of spikes, he takes his rest,
As if it were his house, and I the guest.

The Last of Life

Helen Blackshear
Montgomery, Alabama

Soon I will be among the unlovely old,
dewlapped and wrinkled, bent, and thin of hair
searching in crowds for friends no longer there,
tending a dying fire in rooms grown cold.
I will be cautious where I once was bold.
I will be careful when I climb the stair.
I will count pennies and be slow to share
who flung so joyously my store of gold.

Must I grow old and ugly? Damned if I will!
These are the wiles of my ancient enemy, fear,
probing my armor, prying with bitter knife.
I will not heed his lies. Pray God I may fill
these autumn days so full of warmth and cheer
no ghost will dare to haunt this feast of life.

Checking in and Out

Bonnie Roberts
Huntsville, Alabama

Stand in your bedroom doorway.
Look at how the furniture is arranged.
Ask yourself why the foot of your bed is to the south
instead of to the north.
You can only do this if you can see
the bed as a strange object,
as something you just came upon
in a foreign land.
This helps:
Watch a whale ascend to the surface,
dive into vortex of sky.
When you come back to your bedroom door,
you will be both amazed and horrified
at what you have done to life.
You will see how at one moment,
life became so overly focused
you thought the picture was real
and you climbed into it.

Do this at least:
Make sure you have
chosen
everything.
The bedpost,
the trunk,
the oval mirror.
And if you haven't,
take the room down, board by board,
and build you another,
this time with a window on the sea,
or a hole in the floor for a banyan tree.
Else, go on the road.
Leave safety and warmth behind.
Choose your hills.
Choose your blind turns.
Choose your picture,
knowing it is that.

Just Right

Susan Murphy
Birmingham, Alabama

Ah... the perfect cup of tea. English breakfast tea bag, steeped for four minutes, with clover honey and a slice of lemon. No instant today, no packaged sugar substitute. The tea is not too hot, not too cold. It is, as Goldilocks would say, just right.

If I sound too easily awed, let me tell you that it took me twenty-one years to reach this golden moment. You see, as a teacher-mother-wife-cook-and-bottle washer, my days have been spent hopping up from the table, chasing after homework, answering the phone. There have been meals to serve, little ones to comfort, and uniforms to mend. In between these tasks, I necessarily settled for lukewarm coffee, programs already in progress, and broken cookies. Mama Bear leftovers.

Don't get me wrong. I wouldn't have missed it for the world. Those years held their own reward, to be sure. When you decide to bring children into this world, you trade hot baths and perfectly done steaks for macaroni necklaces and tissue paper corsages. Believe me, it's a good deal.

But now, my life is changing. My children are growing up, grown almost, and I find myself looking down a very different road. It seems like only yesterday I was picking out baby names. Today, I'm preparing to send my youngest daughter off to college. I'm packing up sheets and towels, gathering boxes of Band-Aids® and aspirin tablets, and stockpiling quarters for the soda machines. There will be no family medicine cabinet to fall back on, no refrigerator to raid in the middle of the night.

For the first time, my daughter will be doing her own laundry, ironing her own shirts. Oh my gosh... I never taught her how to iron! What else did I leave out?

I've been through all this packing stuff before, but that doesn't make it any easier. In fact, it may be harder. Two years ago, when I sent my older daughter off to college, I had no inkling how much I would miss her. Now I know. And this time, there won't be another child waiting for me back home, a built-in reason to pull myself together and keep moving. This is the

222   *Ordinary and Sacred As Blood*

end of the line. No more prom dresses, no more school pictures, no more arguing over dinnertime phone calls. No more giggles. From here on in, things could be a little... quiet.

I'm still determined to keep moving, but what's the next step? Get a job? Take a cruise? Join the circus? What do I want to be now that I am grown up? Ironically, I find myself in the same position as my college bound daughter. Well, not quite. I think I'm much better equipped at this point to make such big decisions. I know more about what I want simply because I have eliminated so many things along the way. I've been there and done that, kept what worked and discarded the rest. Now, if I don't want to attend a meeting, I don't go. If I don't like liver, I don't eat it.

But not eating liver isn't a complete blueprint for happiness. There's got to be more. What am I going to do with the rest of my life? I have no idea.

Maybe I'll have some blinding flash of inspiration. Maybe the answer will be revealed to me in a fortune cookie.

For now, however, like an older and wiser Mama Bear, I will leave my future on the table, take a walk in the forest, and mull over the possibilities. And when I come home, I will brew a cup of tea for myself that is not too hot, not too cold, but just right.

I Feel A Change In The Wind

Michelle D. Guyton
Mobile, Alabama

Mama, people talks about me they say I aine gon make it
They talkin bout you now
and when you make it
they're be sayin sumpin else.
you jes keep on working
sumpin gon come d'reckly

Mama Velma misuses her old grandmother tells her lies and steals her
    money
Can't go through life mis'using people
if you do gon find yourself
comin' up on one
side and goin down on the other
you jes keep on workin
sumpin gon come d'reckly

Mama, gotta lot of irons in the fire
but ain't none of them gittin hot
Don't worry God's gon make a way for you
and it's gon be a good one
you jes keep on workin
sumpin gon come d'reckly

A change is comin I can feel it in the wind,
I'm jes keep on workin
sumpin gon come d'reckly

A Blessing for the Journey

Susan Luther
Huntsville, Alabama

> *It is not a stone to skip,*
> *though it is flat and knows joy,*
> *but something to wish upon, to hold.*
> —Jean Burden

Choose something, I say to departing friends.
Take whatever is your will. Stones, shells,

disintegrate of wood, a bit of bark, a sough of cotton,
wave-begotten charms polished

to a calcine silk. Each has its story: this came
from Sanibel, the Outer Banks, Clevedon, Town

Creek, Vermont's Green Mountains, the neighborhood
road I walk. I've harbored it, I explain, in a bowl

of pink Depression glass, on a plate
pressed with flowers & devoted

to the stones of England; atop white tile
in an apothecary jar. Or: it kept time

on my altar, with the swallow-tailed butterfly
in glass that once held bath crystals, still

fragrant when the cork is lifted — the wasps'
nests, a clutch of feathers, red clay,

a maple wand, a sparrow's nest
lined with my own hair.

Signs, all of them,

of all the treasures in the world,
of everything I cannot give,

and of what I have,
and can.

And if I had asked something
to remember you by?

It might be one white hair,
a nation's sorrow in a shard of bone,

a stone with an eye through which
you once spied a calm, then

irascible, sea. None, and all
of these are what I'd choose for you:

something mysterious & familiar, unpossessable
as the ground, a bird, sycamore

holding a full moon beside the creek
in its arms, moon on water, doe

in woods, a firefly's vagrant
light.

Ordinary and Sacred As Blood

"All truths wait in things," Whitman said:

the way birdsong
can measure a heart,

a good meal can speak of more
than substance on the tongue, a fiery

shimmering inhabits
sunlight: the way a word —

blessing — has of siting the quality
of grief and distance, the silent passages

of joy, the way it smooths
to resonance in the soul

like a well-turned stone.

About the Contributors

ASPS   Alabama State Poetry Society
AWC   Alabama Writers' Conclave

Jessie Sherer Abbott is the mother of two sons, Bud and Lee. She retired from Wright-Patterson Air Force Base, Ohio, with 23 years Federal Civil Service. Abbott has had her stories and poetry published in *Leatherneck, Magazine of the Marines, Family Circle Magazine, Wheels of Time Magazine, Reading Our Lives — Participants Anthology* (Auburn University), UAB Walker College's *Voices and Visions for 1995* and *1996, Springfield Daily News, Fairborn Herald, Xenia Gazette, Daily Mountain Eagle* and *Northwest Alabamian.*

Pippa Coulter Abston, a pediatrician and poet, has spent most of her life in Alabama. She placed third in the national 1989 William Carlos Williams contest and first for a contemporary poem entry in the 1998 AWC. Her work has also been included in *Vital Signs,* an anthology of physician-poets and in *Alabama Horizons,* a collection from the Mountain Valley Poets (a group to which she is deeply grateful). She and her husband of fourteen years have two children, Seth and Erin.

Jane Allen was born in Virginia and, after marriage, moved to Alabama. She was an editor/writer for the Air Force for many years, retiring from Federal service in 1994. She enjoys writing fiction, nonfiction, and poetry —and entering contests. Through the years, her works have been included in *Progressive Farmer,* a *Reminisce* book, and various publications of winning entries. Her hobbies are writing, reading and walking. She is the mother of three and grandmother of one.

Janet Anderson is an advertising consultant and freelance writer in the Huntsville market. She has had numerous poems published in a variety of small literary magazines and anthologies, and has been honored by poetry societies for her work. She is married, has two young daughters with special needs and is active in her community as a child and family advocate.

Elsie Walters Azar, a mother of three and former Jazz pianist, began writing non-fiction for trade magazines in 1980. Now she writes fiction, which she says enables her to "cross thresholds and expand boundaries." Among the diverse short stories she has authored are "Press 'F-1' for Help," drama; "The Dead of Winter," suspense; "The Daze of My Life," humor; and *An Ear for Murder,* a mystery novel.

Anne M. Bailey is a free-lance writer, essayist and poet living in Birmingham, Alabama. She is the founder of Wise Word Arts which creates classes, lectures and workshops on topics that stimulate and inspire. She holds a B.A. in Chinese from Barnard College of Columbia University, and an MFA in Book Arts: Bookbinding, from the University of Alabama, Tuscaloosa. She is a single parent unschooling her son, Edward. She loves the wild Alabama woods and playing violin.

Deryl Barnhill is Mom to four children and Oma to six grandchildren. She has moved around the world with her Air Force spouse, who is now retired. She is a retired guidance counselor and currently challenged with the volunteer activity of teaching English to international students. Previous short stories have been recognized by the AWC. Writing is a passion for Deryl who feels honored to have her work included with other Alabama female writers.

Helen F. Blackshear has three daughters, eight grandchildren and fourteen great-grandchildren. She is Poet Laureate of Alabama and her hardback collection of poems, *Alabama Album,* was published in 1997 by Black Belt Press. She is the author of *Creek Captives,* history stories for children, and three books of essays, *Mother was a Rebel, Southern Smorgasboard* and *From Peddler to Philanthopist, the Freidman Story.*

Carolyn Buchanan of Auburn is an award winning short story writer and painter, with three published articles and a one-woman show of pastels and oil paintings. A 'housewife on parole' when she is writing, she manages to work on her novel, a humorous murder mystery, as well as chauffeur, feed and sort of look after her husband Jerry, and sons Bill and B.G. Martha Stewart she is not.

Rusty Bynum has written newspaper and magazine articles, public relations materials, advertising, corporate newsletters, documentary film scripts, biographies, novels, short stories and stage plays. She is now playwright-in-residence for Parnassus Productions. Her latest play, *Legacy of Galileo, An Encounter with Genius* is currently touring the eastern U.S. She lives in Huntsville, Alabama, with her husband Larry Bingham, three dogs, a cat and flocks of wild birds.

Joanne Ramey Cage is an Alabama native, a lifelong writer, and a member of the ASPS. Her poems have been published in journals, newspapers and anthologies. Many, including the selection in this book, have won prizes in state and national competitions. Recently retired, Joanne is happy to have more time to enjoy her hobbies, quilting and painting, and (always) writing.

Carol Case, currently pursuing an M.A. in creative writing at the University of South Alabama, has published poetry in *Astarte, Touchstone,* and *Will Work for Peace: New Political Poems.*

Ramey Channell is a writer and artist. Her poetry has been published by *Scholastic Press, Elk River Review, Tahana Whitecrow Foundation* and the ASPS. "In a Land That Is Fairer Than Day" is her first published short story. She is currently working on children's books, loves teaching children's art and has long been active in Native American affairs.

Jackie Cleveland, a native Kentuckian, has resided in Alabama since 1981. She is the mother of three grown children, who continue to supply poetry material. Her poems have appeared in several publications. Samford University recently published three of her poems in the 1999 spring issue of *Sojourn.* A former schoolteacher, she now leads ladies' Bible studies through her local church.

Ora Dark is the mother of three and married to the hero of her first novel, *No Guts, No Glory,* the story of how she met her prince through Dial-A-Sailor. She writes about everyday life with humor and quirky insight. She teaches a Humor Writing Workshop at Auburn University and has recently branched out into the world of stand-up comedy in Atlanta. Her desire is to become a "cheap, addictive, anti-depressant."

Michele 'chele' Debnam belives art is purest straight from the heart, unspoiled by the hands of others. She is fascinated by history, magic, mythology, the Arts, metal music and role-playing games. Her totem is the cat and many seem to flock around her. She believes we should learn to respect mother nature in all her guises. She is married to a darkly handsome man. She has been published in *A Celebration of Poets* and several times in *Playgrounds* magazine.

Patt M. Devitt is a native Alabamian who raised four children in Tuscaloosa. She recently wrote a series of articles for the Northport Gazette, "Let's Explore...!" encouraging children to explore the historical Northport/Tuscaloosa area. She spends winters at her Lake Tuscaloosa home with Canadian husband Vince and cat Hobbs. In summer, they live at Lake Chemong, Peterborough, Canada.

Estel M. Dodd is the mother of four adult sons and one small granddaughter. A retired classroom teacher, she is a lover of classical music, a singer and former piano teacher. She is a member of the ASPS, the National Federation of State Poetry Societies and the AWC. She was Alabama's Poet of the Year in 1993, the same year that her first book of poetry, *Sunlight and Shadows,* was published.

Marge Edde is a native of Alabama, residing in the Huntsville area for more than 35 years. Her poetry has appeared in several local publications and in *Alabama Horizons,* a collection of works by several North Alabama poets. She and her husband, Ted, have one son, one daughter-in-law and one delightful granddaughter.

Linda Frank is a financial advisor who is also a writer, artist, photographer and calligrapher in her spare time. Her poems have been published in the Huntsville Jazz and Poetry Society - 3rd Annual Celebration. She loves hiking on Monte Sano with her dog, Suneema in Huntsville.

Alison Wright Franks is the epitome of 'been there, done that' bride, mother, divorcee, second-wife, stepmother, widow, mother-in-law and grandmother. This piece, written after the death of her only son, is taken from her memoirs, *Messages for Savannah,* a gift to her granddaughter.

Linda Frost is practically an associate professor of English at the University of Alabama at Birmingham where she teaches creative writing, women's studies and American literature. Her poetry has appeared in *Mudfish, Birmingham Poetry Review, Columbia,* and *Sing Heavenly Muse!* and she has just completed her first collection of poems, *Flexible Cookie.* Although originally from Ohio, Linda is now proud to hail from Birmingham and has even developed a deep love of collard greens.

Elizabeth Frye is a 15-year-old high school student at Jefferson County International Baccalaureate School. Although she has been recognized by several local writing contests, her poem, "Day After Solstice," is her first work to be published. She is extremely delighted to be included among such gifted women at such a young age.

Faye Gaston has published three books of her poetry. She has been a volunteer journalist/photographer for her local newspaper for many years. Retired from the work place, she gives poetry readings at civic clubs and schools. She is a member of the ASPS and was Bullock County "Woman of the Year" in 1993-94. She was inducted into the Robert E. Lee High School Hall of Fame (Montgomery) in 1994 for her contributions as a civic community and religious leader of Bullock County.

Maggie Geist, a graduate of the University of Alabama, was an elementary school teacher for the Tuscaloosa City and County School System for 15 years. During her teaching career, she wrote two children's books, *The*

History of Northport: A Native Son's Story published by Strode Publishing and *The Dreams of a Young Chief, Chief Tuskaloosa* published by Portals Press.

Anne George has never lived anywhere but Alabama. Therefore, she is a graduate of the University of Alabama, has two deviled egg plates and keeps her silver flatware polished. She has received an Individual Fellowship Award from the Alabama State Council on the Arts and three Hackney Awards. Her short stories and poems have been widely published in literary journals and anthologies. Her last volume of poetry, *Some of it is True,* was nominated for the Pulitzer in 1994, the year she was named Poet of the Year by the ASPS. Patricia Anne and Mary Alice, who appear in her Southern Sisters mystery novels (Avon), are her sorority sisters.

Virginia Gilbert has lived in Alabama since 1980. She has a MFA in Creative Writing - Poetry from the Iowa Writers' Workshop and a Ph.D. in English with a Creative Dissertation in Poetry from the University of Nebraska-Lincoln. A returned Peace Corps Volunteer (South Korea), she was evacuated while an English instructor in Iran in February 1979. Currently she is Director of the Program in Creative Writing at Alabama A & M University. She has received a National Endowment for the Arts grant, a Hackney Literary Award, and a Fulbright-Hays Fellowship to the Republic of China. Her books are *That Other Brightness, The Earth Above,* and *To Keep at Bay the Hounds.* Her poetry can be found in the recent anthology, *Claiming the Spirit Within,* and in the upcoming anthology, *Wordslens.*

Kenney Greene is a native of Opelika and has had articles published in genealogy magazines and has written books about her family history. Currently she is writing a novel, *Zelma,* about a woman living in a textile mill village in the 1930s and 1940s. The woman encounters a lot of difficulties but through her strong faith in God overcomes many problems.

Michelle D. Guyton is a mother of two. Her poems have been published in many issues of *Reflections Literary Journal.* She enjoys writing and listening to poetry.

Ruth Thomas Halbrooks has published four books of poetry, has been published over 185 times, and has won over 165 awards. She won the 1988 Poet of the Year award from ASPS, named Distinguished Poet by "Poets at Work" editor, and been voted number one in the nation by subscibers to *Bell's Letters* three times and twice by subscribers to *R.B's Poets' Viewpoint.*

Mary Halliburton has poems and short stories in a variety of publications including Milford Fine Arts Council's *Hightide,* the *California State Poetry*

Quarterly, In Friendship's Garden and *The Quarterly* by Anderie Poetry Press, *Encore 1997 NFSPS Prize Poems, 1997-98 Journal of the Arizona State Poetry Society, WVPS 1996 Winners Anthology, Prize Poems,* 1998 Pennsylvania State Poetry Society, and *Alalitcom,* receiving 1994-97 AWC awards

For **Jan Martin Harris,** the near-death experience of her son was the spark that got her writing. A registered nurse for 24 years, she also married a nurse. She belongs to four writers' groups. Her publishing credits include: *Christian Woman, Lonzie's Fried Chicken, The Alalitcom, ByLine, The Child Times of Alabama, The Child Within, Housewife Writer's Forum,* and *Power for Today.* She's revising her first novel, a suspense. She dreams of writing for a living and traveling.

Tina Harris graduated from the University of Montevallo, and continues her education by living in the small town of Montevallo. For a living, she hangs out with delinquent boys in the woods. She is addicted to throwing pottery and compulsively fills notebooks with ideas. She will write for books!

Kennette Harrison, a tree hugger, a bird-watcher, a story-warrior, writes poetry, reviews, interviews, essays and short stories. She has published in *Prairy Schooner, Southern Humanities Review, Nimrod,* and *Poem.* She is the author of a prize-winning chapbook, *Kitchen Without Precedent,* and a book of poetry, *Dowsing for Light.* She has been the recipient of Hackney awards in short story and poetry. She has a master's degree in Creative Studies from the University of Central Oklahoma.

Jane-Ann Heitmueller and husband, Ray, relish a life of retirement from the field of education on their 126-year-old authentically restored German homeplace, Mulberry Farm. A mood of nostalgia and whimsy permeates the writings of this mother of two sons, as she attempts to reflect upon what are often considered the ordinary, mundane aspects of life, both past and present. Her poetry and short stories have been published in local newspapers, magazines and books.

Rebecca Davis Henderson, a native of Cullman, has lived the past 32 years in Madison with husband Otis and son Lee. As a medical technologist, she served in the Peace Corps in East Africa. Her article "Resurrection" won the 1997 AWC Workshop award. In 1993 she completed a book, *Walter Walker Brown Sr. of Virginia and Tennessee: with allied families.* Plans for a backyard Native American medicine wheel this summer will celebrate the healing energies of Mother Earth.

Dorothy Diemer Hendry moved to Huntsville in 1962 with her engineer husband Wick and their four children. She chaired the Huntsville High English Department and edited teacher's manuals for Harcourt Brace Jovanovich. She writes lyrics for her sister, composer Ema Lou Diemer of Santa Barbara, California. Their publications include anthems, hymns, cantatas, and madrigals. In May, 1999, Central Missouri State University awarded the two sisters honorary Doctors of Letters degrees. She grows 300 varieties of roses. She says, "Naturally we love the miniature named Sweet Home Alabama."

Marilyn Hunt-Lewis, Ed.H, aka N. Naila El-Amin, is a technical writer with more than twenty years experience as an educator. She frequently publishes her poems online in "The Write Brain" and will publish her first complete volume of poetry this summer. The mother of five and grandmother of three, Marilyn holds degrees from Spelman College, Smith College, and the University of Massachusetts. She began winning writing contests at age 14 but mostly enjoys giving her poems to her friends.

Laura Hunter, mother of twins, grandmother of one and kitty-sitter for her son's cat for the past eleven years, lives in Northport with her husband and two cocker spaniels. On retiring from teaching, she began her writing career. She has received several literary awards, including the Birmingham-Southern Hackney Award for poetry and first place in the Scott & Zelda Fitzgerald Museum Association Literary Contest. Her poetry and short stories appear in *Marrs Field Journal, Beyond Doggerel,* and *Belles' Letters.*

Evelyn Hurley lives in Gaylesville, Alabama and has been the librarian/ senior English teacher for 28 years. She is the author of *Girl in the Blue Velvet Swing,* a chapbook of poetry, and has had other poems, articles, essays, short stories and a one-act play published.

Barbara Kaiser, born and raised in Maryland, adopted North Alabama as her retirement home. She is a mother, artist and writer who, for the twenty years before retirement, taught Literature and Creative Writing at the University of Florida. Her work has been published in *Florida Quarterly, Journeying the Way, Florida Living, Brontë Street,* and *Alabama Horizons.*

lauren kenney will graduate from Auburn University in August 1999 with degrees in Theatre and English. Her poems "blind date" and "Pyramids" are her first publications.

Reese Danley-Kilgo, Ph.D., a teacher of education and sociology and counselor of marriage and family for 35 years, is now a writer of poetry, short stories and two novels. She has won many awards and has numerous publications. In her spare time she gardens and grandmothers, plays Scrabble with friends and reviews books for *The Huntsville Times.*

Susan Militzer Luther grew up in Nebraska. But she obeyed the call of her Southern blood and has made her home in Alabama, where the Georgia branch of her family originated, since 1969. Her publications include a chapbook, *Poems on the Line,* a monograph on Coleridge, critical essays and over 150 poems in a variety of journals and anthologies, including *And What Rough Beast: Poems at the End of the Century, Alabama Poets,* and *Alabama Horizons.*

Kelly Magee is graduating summa cum laude from Auburn University in June 1999 with a major in English and a minor in Women's Studies. This is her first publication. Although only a resident of Alabama for three years, she is happy to have a part in such an important and much needed book.

Kimberly D. Martz, currently a student in creative writing at Auburn University, hopes to graduate before pigs learn to fly. She enjoys reading, photography and drawing and drinking iced tea on Sunday afternoons.

Angelynne Amick McMullen (Angie) is currently an at-home mom for her two children, Ryan and Laura. She is also trained as a licensed clinical psychologist and worked in the field of adult traumatic experience for ten years. During the last year, she has been exploring the exciting world of creative writing and has had one poem published in *Sojourn,* Samford University's Journal of Arts and Literature.

B. Kim Meyer has published hundreds of poems in small press, as well as a number of short fiction pieces. She is currently co-editing an ezine called *Scrawl* and works free-lance, designing and setting up websites. Worldnet (AT&T) will be featuring her on November 7th (her birthday), 1999, as writer of the day on their women's calendar. She has been surrounded by incredible people all her life who allow her to be who she is.

Charlotte Miller was born in Roanoke, Alabama, and is a graduate of Auburn University. Her first novel, *Behold, this Dreamer,* scheduled for publication by Black Belt Press in Spring 2000, opens her trilogy of novels about the South which will continue with *Through a Glass, Darkly* and conclude with *There is a River.* She is a certified public accountant and is the mother of ten year old Justin.

Mary Carol Moran's first two novels were published in 1995 and 1997. In 1998, she won two novel awards from the Southeastern Writers

Association. She teaches the Novel Writers' Workshop for the Auburn University Outreach Program, and writes poetry whenever she can. She recently established River's Edge Publishing Company, L.L.C.

Dianna Brown Murphree's calling cards read "Interior Decorator, Entertainer, Gaudy Broad." "Do I dare add Writer?" she asks. Her work has been included in *Reflections, A Poetry Quarterly,* and *The Sampler,* by the ASPS. A novice of two years, she feels tremendously honored to be included in this publication with sister Alabamians. This busy grandmother sings with a band, serves as judge for Miss Alabama and Georgia Pageants, is on the Salvation Army Advisory Council and loves to boogie with husband Melvin at his fraternity dances.

Susan Murphy has been a humor columnist for the *Over the Mountain Journal* in Birmingham since 1990. Her work has also appeared in the *Birmingham News,* the *Atlanta Journal/Constitution* and *Atlanta Parent Magazine.* She is the author of nine humor books, including *Mad Dog Mom,* which won the 1998 Small Press Award for Humor. Susan resides in Birmingham with her husband, two daughters, a naughty dog, a neurotic cat and three nondescript fish.

Helen Norris has published four novels and three collections of short stories, which separately have won a number of awards and been translated into Dutch, Polish, and Chinese. Two have been filmed for TV. A novel won the Pen Women's Bienniel Award. Her books have been finalists for Altantic Monthly Press, PEN/Faulkner, and Los Angeles Times Fiction awards. Two of her books have been club selections. Two poetry collections have been the ASPS Book of the Year.

Georgette Perry, born in Montgomery, is a lifelong Alabamian. Her poetry has appeared in the anthology, *The Unitarian Universalist Poets: A Contemporary American Survey,* and in many magazines, recently in *Cedar Hill Review, Hiram Poetry Review,* and *Lilliput Review.* Since retirement she enjoys taking part in small press activities through her own Catamount Press.

Madge Pfleger, retired professional, shared editorship of *The Representative,* a weekly newspaper, in the post World War II 40s and 50s. Now in her late 70s, she has fond memories of flying and sailing when neither the skies nor the seas were so crowded. Several years ago, her first book of poetry, *Catching Dragonflies,* was published.

Marian Phillips, wife, mother of two, grandmother of three, has written verse all her life, some published. She was a journalist before teaching high school for 26 years and loves to travel to foreign countries. She found many poets in hospitable Huntsville, her new home.

Van Potter is a graduate of Tuskegee University and is working on her master's at Auburn University. She has worked as a copy editor at a newspaper and now is a technical writer in Columbus, Georgia. She loves writing, playing softball and listening to music from the 1960s and 1970s.

Judy Ritter, a retired teacher and grandmother of three, now serves as director of religious education at a large church in Gadsden. She and her husband Andy spend much time at their farm in western Etowah County where she enjoys gardening and hiking. Judy's poetry and short stories have appeared in several publications. She is presently writing a novel based in her native region of South Louisiana.

Bonnie Roberts' first book-length collection of poetry, *To Hide in the Light,* was nominated for a Pulitzer Prize and was awarded Book of the Year by the ASPS. Her work has been published in small press and literary magazines, nationally and internationally, including *Bogg, Croton Review, Kentucky Poetry Review,* and *Poetry Today.* She has received numerous fellowships. Most recently, she won a Fulbright to study in Turkey.

Melissa Roth, a recent graduate of Auburn University with a degree in English/Creative Writing, served as the Assistant Editor of *The Circle,* Auburn's literary magazine, and did research work for books and articles in the field of eighteenth century studies. She is busy receiving her Montessori Teacher Training and looking at graduate schools. Her poem "Prayer for My Grandmother" is her first published piece of work and she is thrilled to join other Alabama women in giving life to their diverse voices.

Evelyn Ryan, mother of three, great-grandmother of seventeen, lives on a country acre at Harvest, Alabama. She has always enjoyed the written word, and has had informal articles and poems published since high school. At age 88, she sews, gardens and paints water colors, and finds life good.

Patricia Sammon has won awards at the state, regional and national level for stories, poetry and a novel. She was graduated from Cornell University, and completed a graduate degree at The Queen's University, in Canada. She is a weekly contributor of essays to her local National Public Radio Affiliate, WLRH, and teaches poetry workshops for The Monte Sano Learning Center. She has been active in human rights work for twenty years. She lives with her family in Huntsville, Alabama.

Alma V. Sanders is a poet, artist, graduate of Middle Tenn. State University, and retired mathematician. She's best known for her humorous writing and standup comedy about unodes, googols, her after-becoming-grandmother adoption. Her "Middle Sister Memories" won MENSA and Alabama Poetry Society awards. Alma has five daughters: 60% grand! She grew up up yonder in Lawrence County, Tennessee. She's an avid traveler, having explored many yonders (out, over, up, down) and beyond there.

Sallie Scott, a 1996 graduate of Athens University and a fifth generation Alabamian, has been published in *The Poetry Guild* of the University of North Alabama, and *The National Library of Poetry.* She writes for her neighborhood newsletter, *LakeLife* and her church publication, *The Messenger.* Recently, her first song was published by the Association of Songwriters and Lyricists. The history of her family and her community, which she is very proud of writing, are in *The Heritage of Madison County, Alabama.*

La Rora Shonnise is a recent graduate of Auburn University. She has written poems for private services and essays for special family occasions. She enjoys nature, dancing, playing the piano and is learning to play the guitar. Aside from English, she speaks Spanish, Japanese and Cherokee. Her poems in this book are her first published work. She is excited to launch her writing career among such talented artists.

Nabella Shunnarah has a master's in English education and works as a free-lance writer and part-time English instructor in colleges and public schools. Her articles and book reviews have appeared in *The Birmingham News, Birmingham Magazine* and *Washington Report on Middle East Affairs.* She is working on children's fiction and a novel about Arab-Americans. She lives in Birmingham with her daughters and a son and his family.

Particia A. Sibley, a former school teacher, has been writing poetry since she was a student. Two of her favorite pastimes are her pet cockatiel, Jingles (who calls her "Mommy"), and volunteering at a nearby Home for the Elderly, where she receives much of her inspiration. Pat's poetry has been published in anthologies, chapbooks, magazines and on cassette tapes.

Frances Cooper Smith published a collection of her poems, *The Words Unsaid,* in 1976. She has been the recipient of several awards from the ASPS and Pen Women. She has two children, is grandmother to five and great-grandmother to six.

Linda Strange's humor articles have been published in *Domestique, Nostalgia, Reminisce, Happiness Magazine, The Huntsville Times, SeniorView* (The

Huntsville Senior Center Magazine), *Northeast Alabama OVERLOOK Magazine* (Albertville), *The Choctaw Advocate* (Butler, Alabama) and *Old Huntsville*. Two of her short humor articles recently won honorable mention in a *ByLine Magazine* writing contest. When she's not writing, Linda cracks jokes and tries her best to make her husband and friends laugh.

Rachel Smith Sykes is a graduate of Mississippi State University and Alabama A&M University. She is a counselor at Grissom High School and is a member of Calhoun College's adjunct faculty. Rachel is secretary of the Echota Cherokee Tribe of Alabama. During breaks she writes, plays the piano and studies Native American literary criticism and languages in Oklahoma.

Natasha Trethewey was born in Gulfport, Mississippi, in 1966. She has received an NEA fellowship, and her poems have appeared in *Agni, The American Poetry Review, Callaloo, Gettysburg Review, The Massachusetts Review, New England Review, North American Review* and *The Southern Review*. She is an assistant professor of English at Auburn University.

Margaret J. Vann, a longtime resident of Huntsville, has been writing since her graduate poetry class with Dr. Mason at UA. Her poems have been published in small magazines, including *The Scribbler, Red Mountain Rendezvous,* and *The Sampler*. She is editor of Historic Huntsville *Quarterly,* a preservation publication. She has a wild(flower) garden, two black cats, four extraordinary grandchildren, and a husband who also writes. She is thrilled to be included in *Ordinary and Sacred As Blood*.

Frances Cleary Wittmeier, a self-educated writer, spent her first 53 years in rural St. Clair County, Alabama. From that background, rich with its characters and environment, her writing finds its wellspring. In essays published in *Grit* and *Reminisce* magazines, as well as her two chapbooks *Where the Killdeer Ran* and *Sequences,* she captures that time and place. A member of both the AWC and ASPS, she has won numerous awards.

Lynne Zielinski enjoys the friendship of her seven adult children, the magical inspiration of 13 grandkids and the loving partnership of her husband of 41 years. Lynne believes life is a gift from God and what we do with it is our gift to God. Her writings can be found in *Chicken Soup for the Pet Lover's Soul, Chocolate for a Mother's Heart, Tears of a Man* and various magazine and anthology publications. She can be reached via e-mail: Excel11047@aol.com.

Notice of Awards and Previous Publication

AWC   Alabama Writers' Conclave
ASPS   Alabama State Poetry Society
NLAPW National League of American Pen Women

Jessie Sherer Abbott, "High Adventure in the Free State of Winston," *Reading Our Lives* (Auburn), *Voices & Visions–1995, Wheels of Time Magazine, Daily Mountain Eagle, Northwest Alabamian*

Jane Allen, "The Medicine Show," AWC 1979 second place award

Elsie Walters Azar, "Anna," *Huntsville Times,* aired on National Public Radio

Deryl F. Barnhill, "Home Alone on Halloween," *First Ladies News,* First Baptist Church of Tuscaloosa

Helen F. Blackshear, "Mammy Was a Slave," *Mother Was a Rebel,* NLAPW 1998 award, "Beauty Shop," *Alabama Album,* Missouri Senior Contest 1998 award, "My Climbing Tree," Jessee Poet Contest award, "Dialogue with Death," *Alabama Album,* NLAPW state contest award, "The Tearing of Lewis," NLAPW Minnesota contest award, "Ma Nature Takes a Twist," *Alabama Album*

Carolyn Brock Buchanan, "Bridges of Glass," *1998 Alalitcom,* AWC Personal Essay 1998 award

Joanne Ramey Cage, "Winter at the Inn," ASPS Lyrical Expressions 1999 award

Ramey Channell, "Golden Trees," ASPS The Eugene Walter Memorial Poetry contest 1999 award

Reese Danley-Kilgo, "Choices," *Alalitcom,* AWC 1996 award

Estel M. Dodd, "Wounded Visitor: World War II," *Alabama Horizons* (Mulberry River Press, Cullman, AL, nominated for ASPS 1999 Book of the Year)

Elizabeth Frye, "Day after Solstice," *Counterpane* (school literary magazine)

Faye Gaston, "Short Childhood, *Union Springs Herald* newspaper, *People Prisms* (1997)

Ruth Thomas Halbrooks, "Gentle With This World," *Alalitcom,* AWC award, *The Sampler* (ASPS), *Bell's Letters, R. B.'s Poets' View Point* (and award), *Poets at Work, Living Streams* (and award)

Tina Harris, "Watering the Sidewalk," *Fester*

Jane-Ann Heitmueller, "Why Granny," *Yesterday's Memories, Alabama Living Magazine, Cullman Times* newspaper, *Cullman Tribune* newspaper, "Grosspapa and the Crow," *Yesterday's Memories*

Rebecca Davis Henderson, "Christmas Chrysalis," *The Huntsville Times* (titled "Christmas-Easter connection brings back memories of joy")

Dorothy Diemer Hendry, "To a Friend Forever," set to music by Emma Lou Diemer, "Final Examination," NLAPW 1997 award

Marilyn Hunt-Lewis, "Rage," *A Collection of Poetry and Prose by the Writers and Artists Association of Huntsville,* 1991

Evelyn Hurley, "Passing the Peace," *Touchstone*

Barbara M. Kaiser, "Last Visit with Your Grandmother," *Alabama Horizons* (Mulberry River Press, Cullman, AL)

Susan Luther, "Red Clay," *Amaryllis*

Mary Carol Moran, "Matruschka Doll," Ohio State Poetry Day award

Helen Norris, "I Remember Trains," "Now We Lay Us Down to Sleep," "Even Sweetly Scattered," "The Needlewomen," "Bamboo," "The Potter," all in *Whatever is Round* (Curbow Publications, 1994)

Georgette Perry, "Caged," *Earth First*

Madge Pfleger, "Recall–The Inexpensive Sport," NLAPW award

Evelyn Ryan, "Winter Warmth," Extension Department, U.S. Agriculture award, "Kudzu Grows Twelve Inches a Day," Huntsville radio station WLRH award

Nabella Shunnarah, "A Picture for Baba," *Reading Our Lives: Southern Autobiography Anthology* (modified version of story)

Linda Strange, "The Day Grandmother and I Repainted Dad's Ford," "Broken Toasters and Burnt Toast," both in *The Huntsville Times*

Natasha Trethewey, "History Lesson," *Callaloo,* "Flounder," *Callaloo,* "White Lies," *Seattle Review,* "Naola Beauty Academy, New Orleans, 1945," *Agni*

Did you enjoy reading this book?
Would you like to be notified
about future publications from River's Edge?

Are you a writer?
Would you like to receive
guidelines for upcoming compilations ?

☐ Add my name to your readers' mailing list.

☐ Add my name to your writers' mailing list.

name: _____

address: _____

_____

phone: _____ fax: _____

e-mail: _____

Please mail or fax this form to

attn: Mary Carol Moran
River's Edge Publishing Company, L.L.C.
907 4th Place SW
LaFayette, AL 36862
fax (334)864-0445

Ordering is Easy!

Credit card orders can be placed by calling
our toll-free number
877-213-5139

or mail this coupon to
River's Edge Publishing Company, L.L.C.
907 4th Place SW
LaFayette, AL 36862

Qty	Title	Price	Total
	Ordinary and Sacred As Blood: *Alabama women speak*	$11.95	
	subtotal		
	Alabama residents add 4% sales tax		
	postage and handling		
	TOTAL		

Please add $2.00 for the first book and $0.75 for each additional
book for postage and handling. Please make all checks payable
to River's Edge Publishing Company, L.L.C.

name _____

address _____

city _____ state _____ zip _____

telephone (_____) _____

photocopying of this page is permitted